Catechism of Catholic Social Teaching

AMINTORE FANFANI

Catechism of Catholic
Social Teaching

Translated by
REVEREND HENRY J. YANNONE

THE NEWMAN PRESS · WESTMINSTER, MARYLAND
1960

8807

The present translation was made from the third edition of
Summula Sociale Secondo l'Insegnamento Pontificio published
by Editrice Studium in Rome.

Nihil obstat: EDWARD A. CERNY, S.S., S.T.D.
Censor deputatus

Imprimatur: FRANCIS P. KEOUGH, D.D.
Archbishop of Baltimore
September 23, 1959

Preface

In 1939, the Catholic Social Guild of Oxford, England, published *A Catholic Guide to Social and Political Action,* prepared by the Reverend C. C. Clump, S.J., and containing ninety questions with answers supplied from encyclical letters and other episcopal documents. The purpose of this work was to guide Catholics with regard to the principles they should hold concerning such subjects as society, the Church, the State, the relations between Church and State, the political activities of citizens and the latter's relations with the government.

Because of my exile, the only copy of the *Guide* in my possession was left in Italy with Professor Giuseppe Dossetti, with whom I had been working assiduously in an effort to point out to responsible Catholics the way to follow upon termination of the war.

But while in exile in Switzerland, in the spring of 1944, I found a copy of Father Clump's *Guide* in a church in Montreux. This inspired me to translate it into Italian, read it and explain it to the Italian military internees at the University Camp at Vevey. The interest with which they received it prompted me to do the same thing for my companions in exile who were attending the courses at the Universities of Murren and Geneva.

Studying the *Guide* convinced me of the worth of Father Clump's idea of presenting the political and social doctrine of the Church in question-and-answer form. But it also revealed the shortcomings of the method used. Thus, abandoning the idea of translating Father Clump's *Guide,* it was thought advisable to rewrite the entire work according to a new method and with full freedom from the original. Hence, while the question-

and-answer form was rigidly adhered to, a greater variety of texts from papal teachings was added in support of the answers given. In this manner, the average person will find in the plain and brief formulae substantially what he might be seeking; while the more learned who wishes to consult the original sources can easily do that because in all cases the names and the authorship of the original documents are indicated at the end of each quotation.

We share with Father Clump the aim of popularizing the social teachings of the popes. In the subjects on which the popes have made no pronouncements, we have, of course, posed no questions, despite the curiosity of the reader or the interest of this author.

Besides improving the method, almost every question proposed in the original work was changed, either by the introduction of new ones or by the elimination of the old ones. In the case of a few questions retained from Father Clump's work, new quotations were used when more appropriate ones were found. In any case, extensive use was also made of papal documents later than 1939. All this has resulted in a considerable increase in the number of questions. Moreover, the documentation was brought up to December 31, 1955, for this, the third edition. A new division into chapters and sections was introduced and their number increased. Furthermore, a number of fundamental religious truths were added as premises for a better understanding of the work. These truths, which are accepted by Catholics, should at least be presupposed by all others.

In conclusion, it is a pleasure to acknowledge our indebtedness to Father Clump for the inspiration and the aid received from his *Guide*. It was not out of a spirit of novelty or of vanity that we did not simply translate it. A desire to make the work more useful prompted us to undertake the harder task of rethinking and reorganizing the original product.

AMINTORE FANFANI

Rome, January 6, 1953

Postulates of Papal Social Teaching

For a better understanding of the contents of this small *summa* of papal social teachings it is necessary to recall certain truths taught by the Catholic Church. These truths, which Catholics readily accept, must be at least hypothetically presupposed by all others if a proper understanding of this book is to be attained by them.

These are the *postulates:*

1. The existence of a Supreme Being, Creator of all things, who directly and indirectly ordained and does ordain them.

2. All created things have, of necessity, the glory of God as their proper end. Living and intelligent creatures (men) attain it by knowing, loving and serving God in this life and sharing His happiness in the next. Non-intelligent living creatures (animals and plants) and inanimate creatures (elements and composites) attain it by *a*) passively obeying the laws of creation; *b*) testifying by their existence to the power of their Creator; *c*) serving as means to the living intelligent creatures.

3. The knowledge of the existence of God and of some laws (natural laws) given by Him is attainable by reason; since his creation, man has possessed such knowledge in sufficient degree.

4. A deeper knowledge of God is obtained through revelation, by which the essence and the attributes of God and divine positive laws were made known. God Himself disclosed such truths to Adam in Paradise and then to the patriarchs and Moses; later, through special messengers—the Prophets, Jesus Christ, His Son, and

the Apostles—revelation came first to the Jews and then to the whole of humanity.

5. Man was endowed by God with a multiplicity of preternatural and natural gifts. But in punishment for his disobedience to a divine command, he was deprived by God of the preternatural gifts of physical immortality and lost full control over his faculties. In a state of degradation as the result of a weakened will and a consequent loosening of his inordinate tendencies, man awaited for thousands of years the coming of a Mediator who would restore him to his Creator's friendship.

6. God the Father permitted His Son, Jesus Christ, to assume human flesh and come into the world (around the middle of the eighth century of Rome), a)to complete the revelation of the essence, attributes, and laws of God; b) to redeem man from sin, through His sacrifice on the Cross; c) to announce and prepare the coming of the Holy Spirit; d) to sanctify man by the institution of the sacraments and the Church.

7. Jesus Christ preached a particular type of doctrine, essentially contained in the books of the New Testament, which completed and sublimated the natural law and the divine positive laws of the Old Testament.

8. Jesus Christ instituted the Church to administer the sacraments, to propagate and preserve His doctrine and to lead all men to heaven.

9. Jesus Christ gave the Church a head in the person of Peter and his lawful successors, and endowed them with the faculty of guiding it in an infallible way and of moderating all its activities.

10. Christians must acknowledge revelation and its custodians; they must conform their entire lives to revealed truths and keep their activities within the limits indicated by such truths.

11. The Church, the pope, the hierarchy, have no particular political or economic program of their own to propose. It is their right and duty, however, to point out and warn the people against certain political and

economic activities which hinder man from achieving his ultimate end because contrary to moral and religious principles.

It is in view of this that the Church and the popes must also concern themselves with political and social questions. And, insofar as they do it to safeguard religion and morals, Catholics have the obligation to accept, observe and defend the Church's teachings.

Papal Documents Quoted in This Work

NOTE: The extracts from the papal documents have been quoted from a variety of sources but can easily be traced to the following ten by means of the initials after the name of each document, which correspond to the following key. Exceptions are plainly labeled in the text proper.

A.P.   America Press, New York, N. Y.

S.W.   *Social Wellsprings*, ed. Husslein; Milwaukee, The Bruce Publishing Company.

N.C.W.C. National Catholic Welfare Conference, Washington, D. C.

P.P.   The Paulist Press, New York, N. Y.

C.M.   *The Catholic Mind*, 70 East 45th St., New York, N. Y.

U.A.   *The Unwearied Advocate*, ed. Yzermans; St. Cloud, Minn., St. Cloud Bookshop.

L.T.   *The London Tablet*.

P.S.   *The Pope Speaks*, 3622 12th St., N.E., Washington, D. C.

A.T.C.   *All Things in Christ*, ed. Yzermans; Westminster, Md., The Newman Press.

H.J.Y.   The translator of this book, who supplied translations of many texts when an official translation was not available.

PIUS IX
Quanta cura, December 8, 1864. (H.J.Y.)

LEO XIII
Inscrutabili Dei consilio (on the evils affecting modern society), April 21, 1878. (S.W.)

Quod apostolici muneris (on Socialism), December 28, 1878. (S.W.)

Arcanum (on Christian marriage), February 10, 1880. (S.W.)

Diuturnum (on civil government), November 29, 1881. (S.W.)

Cum multa (on conditions in Spain), December 8, 1882. (H.J.Y.)

Immortale Dei (on the Christian constitution of States), November 1, 1885. (S.W.)

Pergrata nobis (on the needs of the Church in Portugal), September 14, 1886. (H.J.Y.)

Libertas (on human liberty), June 20, 1888. (S.W.)

Sapientiae christianae (on Christian citizenship), January 10, 1890. (S.W.)

Graves de communi (on Christian democracy), January 18, 1891. (S.W.)

Rerum novarum, (on the rights of capital and labour), May 15, 1891. (S.W.)

Praeclara gratulationis, June 20, 1894. (H.J.Y.)

Permoti nos (on social conditions in Belgium), July 10, 1895. (H.J.Y.)

Letter to the Archbishop of Bogotá, April 6, 1900. (H.J.Y.)

Giunti al venticinquesimo anno, March 19, 1902. (H.J.Y.)

PIUS X

Il fermo proposito (on Catholic Action), June 11, 1905. (A.T.C.)

Inter catholicos, February 20, 1906. (H.J.Y.)

Singulari quadam (on German labour organizations), September 24, 1912. (A.T.C.)

Address to Pilgrims from Milan, April 3, 1913. (H.J.Y.)

BENEDICT XV

Pacem, Dei munus pulcherrimum (on peace and Christian reconciliation), May 23, 1920. (L.T.)

PIUS XI

Ubi arcano (on the peace of Christ in the reign of Christ), December 21, 1922. (S.W.)

Address to Members of Italian Catholic Action, October 30, 1926. (H.J.Y.)

Peculiari quadam, June 24, 1928. (H.J.Y.)

Divini illius magistri (on the Christian education of youth), December 31, 1929. (N.C.W.C.)

Casti connubii (on Christian marriage in our day), December 31, 1930. (S.W.)

Dobbiamo intrattenerla, April 26, 1931. (H.J.Y.)

Quadragesimo anno (on the restoration of the Christian social order), May 15, 1931. (S.W.)

Non abbiamo bisogno (on Catholic Action), June 29, 1931. (N.C.W.C.)

Letter to the Patriarch of Lisbon, November 10, 1933. (H.J.Y.)

Mit brennender Sorge (on the Church in Germany), March 14, 1937. (N.C.W.C.)

Divini Redemptoris (on atheistic Communism), March 19, 1937. (S.W.)

Nos es muy conocida (on religious conditions in Mexico), March 28, 1937. (C.M.)

PIUS XII

Summi Pontificatus (on the unity of human society), October 20, 1939. (A.P.)

Christmas Message, December 24, 1939. (H.J.Y.)

Christmas Message, December 24, 1940. (U.A.)

Message on Pentecost, June 1, 1941. (C.M.)

Christmas Message, December 24, 1941. (U.A.)

Christmas Message, December 24, 1942. (U.A.)

Christmas Message, December 24, 1944. (U.A.)

Address to the Italian Catholic Workers' Association, March 11, 1945. (C.M.)

Message to the People of Rome, March 18, 1945. (C.M.)

Address to the Men of Catholic Action, April 29, 1945. (C.M.)

Address to the Sacred College, June 2, 1945. (C.M.)

Address to the Sacred Roman Rota, October 2, 1945. (C.M.)

Address to Catholic Women, October 21, 1945. (H.J.Y.)

Address to Catholic Men, September 9, 1947. (H.J.Y.)

Address to Italian Workers, October 20, 1947. (C.M.)

Address to Members of the International Trade Convention, March 7, 1948. (U.A.)

Address to the Sacred College, June 2, 1948. (H.J.Y.)

Christmas Message, December 24, 1948. (U.A.)

Address to Catholic Employers, March 7, 1949. (U.A.)

Christmas Message, December 24, 1949. (U.A.)

Christmas Message, December 24, 1951. (U.A.)

Christmas Message, December 24, 1952. (N.C.W.C.)

Address to Italian Workers, May 1, 1953. (N.C.W.C.)

Address to the Italian Catholic Workers' Association, May 14, 1953. (N.C.W.C.)

Address to Members of the Congress of International Penal Law, October 3, 1953. (*U.A.*)

Christmas Message, December 24, 1953. (*U.A.*)

Address to the International Labour Organization, November 20, 1954. (H.J.Y.)

Christmas Message, December 24, 1954. (*C.M.*)

Address to the Italian Catholic Workers' Association, May 1, 1955. (*P.S.*)

Address to the Christian Employers Association of Italy, June 6, 1955. (N.C.W.C.)

Address to Members of the World Petroleum Congress, June 10, 1955. (H.J.Y.)

Address to Railroad Workers of Rome, June 26, 1955. (N.C.W.C.)

Address to Members of the Italian Study Center for International Reconciliation, October 13, 1955. (N.C.W.C.)

Address to Delegates of the United Nations Food and Agricultural Organization, November 10, 1955. (N.C.W.C.)

Christmas Message, December 24, 1955. (N.C.W.C.)

Contents

Preface   v

Postulates of Papal Social Teaching   ix

Papal Documents Quoted in This Work   xiii

Introduction   xxvii

Part One: Man and Society

I. ORIGIN, NATURE AND RIGHTS OF MAN........... 3

  1. What is the origin and nature of man?...... 3

  2. What is the ultimate end of man?.......... 4

  3. In what does the superior dignity of man consist? 4

  4. What rights were bestowed upon man by his Creator? 5

  5. Why has man a right to life, and in what does this right consist?.................. 6

  6. Why does man have a right to achieve his ultimate end, and how can he achieve it?... 7

  7. Why does man have a right to propagate himself, and how can he do this?............. 8

  8. Why has man the right to possess and to use worldly goods? 8

  9. Why does man have the right of association? 10

  10. In regard to whom are the rights of man inalienable? 11

  11. Can man renounce the exercise of the rights given to him by God?.................. 12

  12. What advantages does man obtain from the full fruition of the rights given to him by God? 13

II. Origin, Nature, Ends and Types of Society... 15

13. What is the origin of society? 15

14. In what sense does society have a divine origin? 15

15. What are the duties of society toward God?. 16

16. Is the practice of religion necessary to the perfection of society? 17

17. What is the end of society?............. 17

18. Must man remain in society?............. 18

19. Is collaboration of the individual necessary to the perfecting of society?................ 18

20. Are there various types of society?........ 19

21. With regard to the latitude of their ends how are societies distinguished? 19

22. With regard to the capability of achieving their ends, how are societies distinguished?.. 20

23. As to their nature, how are societies divided? 20

24. Is there any order among the various forms of societies? 21

25. Is there any form of society which must not be confused with other forms, whether natural or conventional? 22

26. Which is the pre-eminent type among natural societies? 23

III. Necessity, Origin, End of Authority and Obedience Required By It................. 25

27. Is authority necessary in society?......... 25

28. Who is the source of authority?.......... 26

29. What current errors exist with regard to the origin of authority?.................... 26

30. What false principles have led to the denial of a divine origin of authority?........... 28

31. What social dangers arise from the denial of a divine origin of authority?............. 29

32. What benefits arise from the doctrine of the divine origin of authority?................ 31

33. Is the doctrine of the divine origin of authority contrary to the human designation of the one invested with authority?.............. 32

34. What is the purpose of authority?.......... 32

35. How is the authority derived from God to be exercised? 33

36. What is the foundation of human laws and whence do they derive their binding force?.. 33

37. Is authority deserving of respect and obedience? 35

38. Is disobedience to authority ever permitted?. 35

39. Is insurrection against authority permissible?. 36

Part Two: The Family Society

IV. THE FAMILY SOCIETY........................ 41

40. What is the family?..................... 41

41. What eternal laws govern the family?....... 42

42. How is the family constituted among Catholics? 42

43. What are the ends of matrimony?......... 43

44. Is there among Christians a matrimony which is not a sacramental union?.............. 45

45. What are the properties of matrimony?..... 45

46. To whom is the discipline concerning matrimony reserved? 47

47. Who regulates the civil effects of matrimony? 47

48. What fallacies exist today with regard to marriage? 48

49. Is the separation of consorts permissible?.... 52

50. Can a true marriage be dissolved?......... 53

51. What evil effects are produced by divorce?.. 53

52. What are the benefits that flow from the indissolubility of matrimony?............... 54

53. What are the guarantees for the well-being of the family? 55

54. To achieve its perfection, does the family

need to be integrated in civil society or the State? 56

Part Three: The State and the Citizen

V. NATURE, ENDS, AND POWERS OF THE STATE...... 61

55. What is civil society or the State?......... 61

56. What is the end of the State?............. 61

57. What is the common good to be attained by the State? 62

58. Within what limits must the State operate so that the common good may be attained?.... 63

59. Does the State have an educational mission? 65

60. Does the State have religious duties of its own? 67

61. Is the State the protector of liberty?........ 69

62. Must the State take care of the citizens' economic welfare? 70

63. By what means can the State procure public prosperity? 72

64. Is there a form of government that is good for all States? 72

65. Under what conditions can a genuinely democratic form of government satisfy present-day needs? 74

66. Are there any forms of government unsuited for the State, as the instrument through which the common good is attained?............. 75

67. Are there any guarantees against the arbitrary exercise of power on the part of the State?... 78

VI. THE CITIZEN IN PUBLIC LIFE.................. 81

68. Must the citizen take an active part in public life? 81

69. Does a Catholic citizen have a particular obligation to take active part in public life?.... 82

70. With what purpose in view must Catholics take an active part in public life?.......... 83

71. How shall Catholics take an active part in public life? 83

72. What evil would the abstention of Catholics from public life produce? 85

73. In the present conditions, by what directives must the public activities of a citizen be inspired? 86

74. Is the existence of many parties lawful?..... 87

75. What is the position of the Church with reference to political parties? 88

76. May Catholics belong to any political party?. 89

77. Do elected officials and public administrators have any special duties? 90

Part Four: The Church and Its Relations with the State

VII. NATURE, ENDS AND POWERS OF THE CHURCH.... 95

78. What is the Church?.................... 95

79. What is the end of the Church?........... 96

80. Is the Church supreme in its own sphere of operation? 96

81. Does the Church have care only of the supernatural happiness of man? 97

82. What are the rights of the Church?........ 98

83. Why does the Church concern itself with social and economic questions?............ 99

84. Why does the Church concern itself with political questions? 101

85. Can the Church flourish under any form of government? 103

VIII. RELATIONS BETWEEN CHURCH AND STATE...... 105

86. Are the Church and the State supreme in their own respective orders?.............. 105

87. Is collaboration between Church and State natural and necessary? 106

88. Does the State have any duties toward the Church? 108

89. Can the Church remain indifferent to the laws of the State? 108

90. In order to prevent conflicts, can the respective jurisdictions of the Church and the State be determined? 109

91. Are there any fields of jurisdiction common to the Church and the State?............... 109

92. What are the most important cases of mixed jurisdiction? 110

93. Is harmony between the two powers possible even in matters of mixed jurisdiction?...... 111

94. In our times, how is collaboration between Church and State regulated?.............. 111

95. What are the current errors with regard to relations between Church and State?....... 112

96. What are the effects of an erroneous doctrine regarding relations between Church and State? 114

Part Five: The Economic Order

IX. ASPECTS AND CAUSES OF THE PRESENT ECONOMIC DISORDER........................ 119

97. Is the present economic order in keeping with the rights of the individual and the common good? 119

98. What factors have produced the contemporary economic disorder? 121

X. REMEDIES WHICH FURTHER AGGRAVATE THE CONTEMPORARY ECONOMIC DISORDER........... 125

99. Can recourse to free competition or to monopolies heal the inequalities characteristic of the contemporary economic disorder? 125

100. Can the good of the individual and of society be attained by an economic reorganization based on a materialistic concept of life?..... 126

101. Can a new social order be established separately from a religious and moral reform?.... 130

XI. THE CHURCH AND THE REORGANIZATION OF THE ECONOMIC LIFE......................... 133

102. Does the Church have any criteria to offer toward the reorganization of economic life?.. 133

103. What does the action of the Church in the economic field consist in? 134

104. What will happen if the findings and the counsels of the Church are disregarded?.... 135

XII. NATURAL CHARACTERISTICS OF THE ECONOMIC ORDER.......................... 137

105. Can a reorganization of the economic life ignore the natural inequalities among men?.. 137

106. Is the right to private ownership a natural right? 138

107. What is the end of labour?.............. 140

108. Is the right of hereditary transmission of one's goods inherent to the natural right of ownership? 141

109. Is the content of the natural right of ownership the same with all the various peoples?.. 141

110. Does ownership have a social function?..... 143

111. Does one lose the right of ownership by the bad use of property?................... 144

112. What must be man's attitude with regard to riches? 146

113. Is there an insurmountable conflict between the rich and the poor, and capital and labour? 147

114. What are the duties in justice of capitalist employers toward employees and of employees toward their capitalist employers?... 148

115. What is the purpose of organized labour?.... 150

116. Is the wage contract by its very nature unjust? 151

117. What are the characteristics of a just wage?.. 151

118. What is the purpose of the economic activity of a people? 153

119. Can the rationalization of economic life take place spontaneously? 154

XIII. COUNSELS OF THE CHURCH FOR THE REFORMING OF INSTITUTIONS AND PRACTICES IN THE ECONOMIC FIELD 157

120. What is needed for a rationalization of economic life for its human ends? 157

121. Does the reorganization of economic life require the rejection of technical progress? 157

122. Who must attend to the reforming of institutions? 158

123. How will the State attend to the reorganization of economic life? 159

124. May the State intervene to regulate and promote production? 160

125. Does the reform of institutions include also the reform of the right of private ownership? 162

126. May the ownership of certain goods be assigned to the collectivity? 164

127. Is the socialization of business enterprises to be permitted? 164

128. Is the State's intervention in the matter of the distribution of wealth necessary and effective? 165

129. Should the State show any particular interest in the working class? 167

130. Does the State alone have the capability of reorganizing economic life? 171

131. Must the economy of a nation be run along democratic lines? 173

132. Is international cooperation necessary for the reorganization of economic life? 174

133. Must a renewal of morals go together with the reform of institutions? 175

Part Six: International Society

XIV. THE HUMAN COMMUNITY.................... 179

   134. Is there a human society?................ 179

   135. What is the end of human society?......... 179

   136. Does human society have its laws by which it is governed? 180

   137. Is the unity of human society broken by the evolution, the differentiation and the organization of individual peoples into States?...... 181

   138. Does Christian doctrine strengthen the community of mankind? 181

   139. Does love of country exclude love of mankind? 182

XV. INTERNATIONAL ORGANIZATION AND PEACE..... 185

   140. What are the principal dangers militating against a sound human society?........... 185

   141. Is "Cold War" a dangerous condition?...... 186

   142. What are the essential prerequisites for a lasting peace? 188

   143. What are the conditions for the restoration of a new international order?............. 189

   144. What must be the aim of a new international order? 191

   145. Is the constitution of an association of nations a desirable thing? 192

   146. Does a society of nations require a common authority? 193

   147. Is European unity desirable?.............. 193

   148. Is a war of aggression a suitable means of solving international controversies?......... 195

INDEX 197

Introduction

Father Yannone's translation of Professor Fanfani's "catechism" of Catholic social teaching fills a real need and will be welcomed, I am sure, by the growing number of American priests and laymen who are zealously working in the ever-expanding field of adult education. It would be difficult to name another publication which provides as good a summary of Catholic social teaching and as much pertinent documentation from papal sources within such a limited number of pages.

Professor Fanfani's credentials speak for themselves. He is an internationally recognized authority on Catholic social teaching and a highly successful practitioner in the field of Catholic social action. In short, he knows what he is talking about. While it is true that in certain particulars his terminology and his approach to contemporary social and economic problems are, understandably, more European than American, that in itself does not detract from the value and the usefulness of his "catechism" for American readers. With a minimum of effort it can readily be adapted to American needs.

RIGHT REV. MSGR. GEORGE G. HIGGINS
Director, Social Action Department, National Catholic Welfare Conference, Washington, D. C.

Part One

Man and Society

Chapter I. *Origin, Nature and Rights of Man*

Chapter II. *Origin, Nature, Ends and Types of Society*

Chapter III. *Necessity, Origin, End of Authority and Obedience Required by It*

CHAPTER I

Origin, Nature and Rights of Man

1

Q. *What is the origin and nature of man?*

A. Man is a being created by God. He is composed of a body which is material and mortal, and of a soul which is spiritual and immortal. He is endowed with intelligence and free will. Through sanctifying grace he is elevated to the dignity of a child of God.

PIUS XI: "Man has a spiritual and immortal soul. He is a person, marvelously endowed by his Creator with gifts of body and mind." *Divini Redemptoris*, p. 351, #27.

PIUS XI: "Only man, the human person, . . . is endowed with reason and a morally free will." *Divini Redemptoris*, p. 352, #29.

LEO XIII: "Liberty, nature's most exalted gift, the endowment of intellectual and rational beings only, confers on man the dignity of abiding 'in the hand of his counsel,' of having power over his own actions." *Libertas*, p. 115, #1.

PIUS XI: "[Man] by sanctifying grace is raised to the dignity of a son of God, and incorporated into the kingdom of God in the Mystical Body of Christ." *Divini Redemptoris*, p. 351, #27.

the right to conjugal and domestic society; the right to work, as the indispensable means towards the maintenance of family life; the right to free choice of a state of life, and hence, too, of the priesthood or religious life; the right to the use of material goods in keeping with his duties and social limitations." *Christmas Message, 1942.*

5

Q. *Why has man a right to life, and in what does this right consist?*

A. In creating man, God conferred upon him the right to life. This becomes a concrete reality in the right to his physical integrity and to a physical, intellectual and moral development and also in the right to obtain normally through his work the means necessary to such development. In the absence of such means his right to life would be a mere theoretical concession.

PIUS XI: "Public magistrates have no direct power over the bodies of their subjects; therefore, where no crime has taken place and there is no cause present for grave punishment, they can never directly harm, or tamper with the integrity of the body." *Casti connubii,* p. 148, #70.

"Private individuals have no other power over the members of their bodies than that which pertains to their natural ends; and they are not free to destroy or mutilate their members, or in any other way render themselves unfit for their natural functions, except when no other provision can be made for the good of the whole body." *Casti connubii,* p. 149, #71.

PIUS XII: "To the personal duty to labor imposed by

nature corresponds and follows the natural right of each individual to make of labor the means to provide for his own life and that of his children." *Address on Pentecost,* 1941.

Pius XII: Man has "the right to maintain and develop his corporal, intellectual, and moral life and especially the right to religious formation and education." *Christmas Message,* 1942.

6

Q. *Why does man have a right to achieve his ultimate end, and how can he achieve it?*

A. Having assigned to him an ultimate end, God has conferred upon him also the right to tend toward it, using the means necessary to its achievement, and practicing freely public and private worship.

Leo XIII: "To contemplate God and to tend to Him is the supreme law of the life of man." *Sapientiae christianae,* p. 143, #1.

Pius X: "No matter what the Christian does, even in the realm of temporal goods, he cannot ignore the supernatural good. Rather, according to the dictates of Christian philosophy, he must order all things to the ultimate end, namely, the Highest Good." *Singulari quadam,* p. 2.

Pius XI: "The true Christian must live a supernatural life in Christ and display it in all his actions." *Divini illius magistri.*

Leo XIII: "Every man in the State may follow the will of God and, from a consciousness of duty and free from every obstacle. . . . This, indeed, is true liberty, a liberty worthy of the sons of God." *Libertas,* p. 133, #21.

Q. *Why does man have a right to propagate himself, and how can he do this?*

A. Having given to man the capacity to propagate himself and the task to perpetuate the human species, God gave him the right to join in marriage and to use it according to the law of nature.

LEO XIII: "No human law can abolish the natural and primitive right of marriage, or in any way limit the chief and principal purpose of marriage, ordained by God's authority from the beginning: 'Increase and multiply.'" *Rerum novarum*, p. 173, #9.

PIUS XI: "The Creator of the human race Himself . . . in His goodness wished to use men as His helpers in the propagation of life. . . . Christian parents must also understand that they are destined . . . to propagate and preserve the human race on earth." *Casti connubii*, p. 129, #12; p. 130, #14.

There exists "the natural and primeval right of marriage." *Casti connubii*, p. 128, #9.

"It is wrong to brand men with the stigma of crime because they contract marriage, on the ground that, despite the fact that they are in every respect capable of matrimony, they will give birth only to defective children, even though they use all care and diligence." *Casti connubii*, p. 148, #69.

Q. *Why has man the right to possess and to use worldly goods?*

A. In giving to man the capacity to produce new things, useful in the achievement of his ultimate end, God gave him the right to possess and to use such things.

Leo XIII: "When man thus spends the industry of his mind and the strength of his body in procuring the fruits of nature, by that act he makes his own that portion of nature's field which he cultivates—that portion on which he leaves, as it were, the impress of his own personality; and it cannot but be just that he should possess that portion as his own, and should have a right to keep it without molestation." *Rerum novarum*, p. 172, #7.

Pius XI: "The right to own private property has been given to man by nature, or rather by the Creator Himself. By means of it, the goods which the Creator has destined for the human race may truly serve this purpose." *Quadragesimo anno*, p. 193, #45.

Pius XI: "The only form of labor, however, which gives the workingman a title to its fruits is that which a man exercises as his own master, and by which some new form or new value is produced." *Quadragesimo anno*, p. 196, #52.

Pius XII: "The dignity of the human person, then, requires normally as a natural foundation of life the right to the use of the goods of the earth. To this right corresponds the fundamental obligation to grant private ownership of property, if possible to all. Positive legislation regulating private ownership may change and more or less restrict its use. But if legislation is to play its part in the pacification of the community, it must prevent the worker, who is or will be a father of a family, from being condemned to an economic dependence and slavery which is irreconcilable with his rights as a person. Whether this slavery arises from the exploitation of private capital or from the power of the State, the result is the same." *Christmas Message*, 1942.

Q. *Why does man have the right of association?*

A. In creating man in need of other men's help, God gave him the right to associate with them, in order to integrate his own inadequacies with others and reach his own perfection.

LEO XIII: "Man's natural instinct moves him to live in civil society. Isolated, he cannot provide himself with the necessary requirements of life, nor procure the means of developing his mental and moral faculties. It is, therefore, divinely ordained that he should lead his life—be it domestic, social, or civil—in contact with his fellow men." *Immortale Dei*, p. 66, #2.

LEO XIII: "The experience of his own weakness urges man to call in help from without. . . . It is this natural impulse which unites men in civil society; and it is this also which makes them band themselves together in associations of citizen with citizen; associations which, it is true, cannot be called societies in the complete sense of the word, but which are real societies nevertheless." *Rerum novarum*, p. 196, #37.

"Particular societies, then, although they exist within the State, and are each a part of the State, nevertheless cannot be prohibited by the State absolutely and as such. For to enter into a 'society' of this kind is the natural right of man. The State must protect natural rights, not destroy them. If it forbids its citizens to form associations, it contradicts the very principle of its own existence; for both they and it exist in virtue of the same principle; viz., the natural propensity of man to live in society. There are times, no doubt, when it is right that the law should interpose to prevent association; as when men join together for purposes which are evidently bad, unjust, or dangerous to the State. In such cases the public authority may justly forbid the formation of associations, and may dissolve them when they already exist. But every precaution should be taken not to violate the rights of individuals, and not to make unreasonable regulations under the pretense of public benefit." *Rerum novarum,* p. 197, #38.

"All such societies are not merely free to exist, but have the further right to adopt such rules and organizations as may best conduce to the attainment of their objects." *Rerum novarum,* p. 200, #42.

10

Q. *In regard to whom are the rights of man inalienable?*

A. All the rights given to man by God are inalienable with regard to other men, whether taken individually or united in a group, and nobody has the right to take them away from him.

Leo XIII: "The fact is that in the projects and enactments of men there exists no power that can change the character and tendency given to things by nature." *Arcanum,* p. 40, #18.

Leo XIII: "The State must protect natural rights, not destroy them." *Rerum novarum,* p. 197, #38.

Leo XIII: "The liberty of those who are in authority does not consist in the power to lay unreasonable and capricious commands upon their subjects . . . but instead the binding force of human laws lies in the fact that they are to be regarded as applications of the eternal law. . . ." *Libertas,* p. 121, #7.

Pius XI: "Society . . . cannot defraud man of his God-granted rights . . . nor . . . by making their use impossible." *Divini Redemptoris,* p. 352, #30.

Pius XII: "Before the state everyone has the right to live honorably his own personal life in the place and under the conditions in which the designs and dispositions of Providence placed him." *Christmas Message,* 1944.

11

Q. *Can man renounce the exercise of the rights given to him by God?*

A. Only in view of a higher perfection, man can renounce the exercise of those natural rights which do not constitute at the same time a duty for him. For instance, for the love of God, he may renounce marriage and the enjoyment of material goods, but he cannot renounce the duty to pursue his ultimate end.

Leo XIII: "No man may outrage with impunity that human dignity which God Himself treats with reverence, nor stand in the way of that higher life which is the preparation for the eternal life of heaven. Nay, more; a man has here no power over himself. To consent to any treatment which is calculated to defeat the end and purpose of his being is beyond his right; he cannot give up his soul to servitude; for it is not man's own rights which are here in question, but the duties towards God, most sacred and inviolable." *Rerum novarum,* p. 190, #32.

Leo XIII: "It is a sin to disobey God for the sake of pleasing men." *Sapientiae christianae,* p. 146, #3.

Leo XIII: "In choosing a state of life, it is indisputable that all are at full liberty either to follow the counsel of Jesus Christ as to virginity, or to enter into the bonds of marriage." *Rerum novarum,* p. 173, #9.

Leo XIII: "The preservation of life is the bounden duty

of each and all, and to fail therein is a crime." *Rerum novarum*, p. 193, #34.

12

Q. *What advantages does man obtain from the full fruition of the rights given to him by God?*

A. Full fruition of the rights given to man by God permits him to use integrally all his faculties, to exploit fully to his own advantage and that of society all the talents received, thus achieving his own end and giving God a more perfect glory.

LEO XIII: "It was divinely ordained that things instituted by God and by nature should be proved by us to be the more profitable and salutary the more they remain unchanged in their full integrity." *Arcanum*, p. 36, #13.

PIUS XI: "For according to Christian doctrine, man, endowed with a social nature, is placed here on earth in order that, spending his life in society and under an authority ordained by God, he may develop and evolve to the full all his faculties to the praise and glory of his Creator; and that, by fulfilling faithfully the duties of his station, he may attain to temporal and eternal happiness." *Quadragesimo anno*, p. 221, #118.

CHAPTER II

Origin, Nature, Ends and Types of Society

13

Q. *What is the origin of society?*

A. Natural instinct and a need for well-being and perfection caused man to unite with other men. Thus society arose.

Leo XIII: "Man's natural instinct moves him to live in civil society. Isolated, he cannot provide himself with the necessary requirements of life, nor procure the means of developing his mental and moral faculties. It is, therefore, divinely ordained that he should lead his life—be it domestic, social, or civil—in contact with his fellow men, where alone his several wants can be adequately supplied." *Immortale Dei*, p. 66, #2.

14

Q. *In what sense does society have a divine origin?*

A. Since God gave man instincts, assets and insufficiencies which move him to unite in a society, it can be said that society was willed and ordained by God himself.

Leo XIII: "And indeed nature, or rather God who is the author of nature, wills that man should live in a civil society; and this is clearly shown both by the faculty of language, the greatest medium of intercourse, and by numerous innate desires of the mind, and the many necessary things, and things of great importance, which men isolated cannot procure, but which they can procure when joined and associated with others." *Diuturnum,* p. 52, #7.

15

Q. *What are the duties of society toward God?*

A. In view of its origin and end, society must recognize God as its author, respect His laws and honor Him.

Leo XIII: "The State . . . must evidently act up to the manifold and weighty duties linking it to God, by the public profession of religion. Nature and reason, commanding every individual devoutly to worship God in holiness . . . bind also the civil community by a like law. For men living together in society, no less than individuals, owe gratitude to God. It is He who gave it being and maintains it, and whose ever-bounteous goodness enriches it with countless blessings." *Immortale Dei,* p. 68, #3.

Leo XIII: "If then any State aims only at external advantage and wealth, it is wont in its government to put God and the moral law aside, it wrongfully turns away from its end and from the teaching of nature, and cannot be called a community or society, but is rather a deceitful resemblance and a parody." *Sapientiae christianae,* p. 143, #2.

Pius XII. "A social teaching or a social reconstruction program which denies or prescinds from this internal relation to God of everything that regards men, is on a false course; and while it builds up with one hand, it prepares with the other the material which sooner or later will undermine and destroy the whole fabric." *Christmas Message,* 1942.

Q. *Is the practice of religion necessary to the perfection of society?*

A. The virtues of self-denial, justice, brotherhood and charity which man needs in associating with others and which cooperate in the perfection of society, find in religion an enhancing and a strengthening force, so that the better the practice of true religion, the more perfect will society also be.

PIUS IX: A society of men free from religious obligations and duties of true justice, can have no other aim except to acquire and accumulate wealth, and no other law in its operations except to follow its indomitable desire to satisfy its own pleasures and convenience." *Quanta cura.*

16

Q. *What is the end of society?*

A. The end of every society, as a medium necessary or optional, is the perfection of man and the common good.

PIUS XI: "In the plan of the Creator, society is a natural means which man can and must use to reach his destined end. Society is for the man and not vice versa. This must not be understood in the sense of liberalistic individualism, which subordinates society to the selfish use of the individual; but only in the sense that by means of an organic union with society and by mutual collaboration the attainment of earthly happiness is placed within the reach of all." *Divini Redemptoris,* p. 352, #29.

Leo XIII: "For nature has not formed society in order that man might look to it as an end, but in order that in it and through it he might find fitting help to his own perfection." *Sapientiae christianae*, p. 143, #2.

Pius XII: "The origin and the primary scope of social life is the conservation, development and perfection of the human person, helping him to realize accurately the demands and values of religion and culture set by the Creator for every man and for all mankind, both as a whole and in its natural ramifications." *Christmas Message*, 1942.

18

Q. *Must man remain in society?*

A. Man must belong to those forms of society which are necessary for the achievement of his perfection.

Pius XI: "But God has likewise destined man for civil society according to the dictates of his very nature. . . . It is society which affords the opportunities for the development of all the individual and social gifts bestowed on human nature. These natural gifts have a value surpassing the immediate interests of the moment, for in society they reflect the divine perfection, which would not be true were man to live alone." *Divini Redemptoris*, p. 352, #29.

19

Q. *Is collaboration of the individual necessary to the perfecting of society?*

A. In order to offset the insufficiencies of man it is necessary that every individual be a part of society, collaborating with the perfecting of society for his own good, for the welfare of mankind and the realization of the plan of Divine Providence.

PIUS XI: "Man cannot be exempted from his divinely imposed obligations toward civil society, and the representatives of authority have the right to coerce him when he refuses without reason to do his duty." *Divini Redemptoris*, p. 352, #30.

20

Q. *Are there various types of society?*

A. Man joins other men for a variety of reasons. The limits, the nature, and the purpose of these groups determine the different types of society.

LEO XIII: "The experience of his own weakness urges man to call in help from without. . . . It is this natural impulse which unites men in civil society; and it is this also which makes them band themselves together in associations of citizen with citizen; associations which, it is true, cannot be called societies in the complete sense of the word, but which are real societies nevertheless. These lesser societies and the society which constitutes the State differ in many things, because their immediate purpose and end is different." *Rerum novarum*, p. 196, #37.

21

Q. *With regard to the latitude of their ends how are societies distinguished?*

A. With regard to the latitude of their ends, societies are universal, such as civil society; and particular or private, such as commercial societies.

LEO XIII: Various societies "differ in many things,

because their immediate purpose and end are different. Civil society exists for the common good, and, therefore, is concerned with the interests of all in general, and with the individual interests in their due place and proportion. Hence, it is called *public* society. . . . But the societies which are formed in the bosom of the State are called *private*, and justly so, because their immediate purpose is the private advantage of the associates. 'Now, a private society,' says St. Thomas again, 'is one which is formed for the purpose of carrying out private business; as when two or three enter into partnership with the view of trading in conjunction.'" *Rerum novarum*, pp. 196 and 197, #37.

22

Q. *With regard to the capability of achieving their ends, how are societies distinguished?*

A. With regard to the capability of reaching their ends, societies are perfect, such as the Church and the State; and imperfect, including all others.

Pius XI: "The Church . . . [is] a perfect society, because it has in itself all the means required for its own end. The civil society is a perfect society having in itself all the means for its own end." *Divini illius magistri.*

23

Q. *As to their nature, how are societies divided?*

A. As to their nature, societies are *natural*, such as the family and civil society; *conventional*, such as cultural, commercial, athletic and the like; and *supernatural*, such as the Church. The supernatural society and the natural are necessary societies.

Pius XI: "There are three necessary societies, distinct from one another and yet harmoniously combined by God, into which man is born: two, namely the family and civil society, belong to the natural order; the third, the Church, to the supernatural order." *Divini illius magistri.*

24

Q. *Is there any order among the various forms of societies?*

A. The order among the various forms of societies depends upon their necessity and the priority of the end of each of them.

Leo XIII: "Particular societies, then, although they exist within the State, and are each a part of the State, nevertheless cannot be prohibited by the State absolutely and as such. For to enter into a 'society' of this kind is the natural right of man. The State must protect natural rights, not destroy them. If it forbids its citizens to form associations, it contradicts the very principle of its own existence; for both they and it exist in virtue of the same principle, viz., the natural propensity of man to live in society. There are times, no doubt, when it is right that the law should interpose to prevent association; as when men join together for purposes which are evidently bad, unjust, or dangerous to the State. In such cases the public authority may justly forbid the formation of associations, and may dissolve them when they already exist. But every precaution should be taken not to violate the rights of individuals, and not to make unreasonable regulations under the pretense of public benefit." *Rerum novarum,* p. 197, #38.

Leo XIII: Ecclesiastic and civil society "each in its kind is supreme. . . . But inasmuch as each of these two powers has authority over the same subjects . . . God . . . has marked out the course of each in right correlation to the other . . . a certain orderly connection, which may be compared to the union of the soul and body in man. The nature and scope of that connection can be determined only . . . by having regard to the nature of each power, and by taking account of the relative excellence and nobleness of their purpose." *Immortale Dei,* pp. 71 and 72, #6.

Leo XIII: "The family [is] . . . a society limited indeed in numbers, but a true 'society,' anterior to every kind of civil society, with rights and duties of its own, totally independent of the commonwealth. . . . Wherefore, provided the limits be not transgressed which are prescribed by the very purposes for which it exists, the family has, at least, equal rights with the State in the choice and pursuit of those things which are needful to its preservation and its just liberty . . . and . . . if a family finds itself in great difficulty . . . it is right that extreme necessity be met by public aid. In like manner, if within the walls of the household there occur grave disturbances of mutual rights, the public power must intervene. . . ." *Rerum novarum,* pp. 173 and 174, #9 and #11.

25

Q. *Is there any form of society which must not be confused with other forms, whether natural or conventional?*

A. The Church, or society of the faithful, on account of its origin, scope and its means, is a perfect society of a supernatural and universal order. It is clearly distinct from all other forms of human societies and possesses its own independence and its own rights.

Pius XI: "The third society, into which man is born when through Baptism he reaches the divine life of grace is the Church; a society of the supernatural order and of universal extent; a perfect society, because it has in itself all the means required for its own end, which is the eternal salvation of mankind; hence it is supreme in its own domain." *Divini illius magistri.*

26

Q. *Which is the pre-eminent type among natural societies?*

A. In view of the universality of its scopes, civil society or the State is a pre-eminent form of society with respect to all other natural and conventional societies. However, this pre-eminence must not infringe upon the rights and prerogatives proper to other forms of society.

Pius XI: "Civil society is a perfect society, having in itself all the means for its peculiar end, which is the temporal well-being of the community, and so, in this respect, that is, in view of the common good, it has pre-eminence over the family, which finds its own suitable temporal perfection precisely in civil society." *Divini illius magistri.*

Pius XI: "The State, then, should leave to these smaller groups the settlement of business problems of minor importance. . . . The more faithfully this principle of 'subsidiary' function is followed, and a graded hierarchical order exists between the various associations, the greater also will be both social authority and social efficiency. The happier, too, and more prosperous will be the condition of the commonwealth." *Quadragesimo anno,* p. 207, #80.

CHAPTER III

Necessity, Origin, End of Authority and Obedience Required By It

27

Q. *Is authority necessary in society?*

A. In order that the members of society may move effectively and unitedly toward the common end, it is necessary to have an authority governing them.

LEO XIII: "In every association and community of men necessity itself compels that some should hold preeminence; lest society, deprived of a prince or head, by which it is ruled, should come to dissolution and be prevented from attaining the end for which it was created and instituted." *Diuturnum* p. 50, #3.

LEO XIII: "But now, a society can neither exist nor be conceived in which there is no one to govern the wills of individuals, in such a way as to make, as it were, one will out of many, and to impel them rightly and orderly to the common good." *Diuturnum*, pp. 52 and 53, #7.

LEO XIII: "But no society can remain united without someone in command, directing all to strive earnestly for the common good. Hence, every civilized community must have a ruling authority. . . ." *Immortale Dei*, p. 66, #2.

PIUS XII: "The democratic state, whether it be monarchial or republican, should, like any other form of government, be entrusted with the power to command with real and effective authority. . . . And if men, using their professional liberty, were to deny all dependence on a superior authority possessing coercive power, they could by this very fact cut the ground from under their own dignity and liberty—by violating, that is, the absolute order of beings and purposes. *Christmas Message,* 1944.

28

Q. *Who is the source of authority?*

A. Since authority is necessary to the life of society, God, who willed society, is the source of all authority.

Leo XIII: "Hence, every civilized community must have a ruling authority, and this authority, no less than society itself, has its source in nature, and consequently has God for its author. It follows, then, that all public power must proceed from God: for God alone is the true and supreme Lord of the world. Everything, without exception, must be subject to Him, and must serve Him, so that whosoever holds the right to govern, holds it from one sole and single source, namely, God, the Sovereign Ruler of all. 'There is no power but from God' (Rom. 13:1)." *Immortale Dei,* p. 66, #2.

Pius XII: "The dignity of political authority is the dignity deriving from its sharing in the authority of God." *Christmas Message,* 1944.

29

Q. *What current errors exist with regard to the origin of authority?*

A. It is erroneously believed that authority was

derived from a free pact entered into at the beginning of society, or that authority resides in the people, or that authority cannot come from God since there is no divine law.

Leo XIII. "Those who believe civil society to have arisen from the free consent of men, looking for the origin of its authority from the same source, say that every person has put himself into the power of the one man in whose person the whole of those rights has been centered. But it is a great error not to see, what is manifest, that men, as they are not a nomad race, have been created, without their own free will, for a natural community of life. It is plain, moreover, that the agreement which they allege is openly a falsehood and a fiction, and that it has no authority to confer on political power such great force, dignity, and firmness as the safety of the State and the common good of the citizens require." *Diuturnum*, p. 53, #8.

Leo XIII: The error of the rationalists "which falsely usurps to itself the name of reason, as it lures and whets the appetite of excelling which man naturally possesses, and gives loose rein to unlawful desires of every kind, has easily penetrated not only the minds of a great multitude of men but to a wide extent civil society also. . . . It has been given out that public authority neither derives its principle, nor its majesty, nor its power of governing from God, but rather from the multitude, which, thinking itself absolved from all divine sanction, bows only to such laws as it shall have made at its own will." *Quod apostolici muneris*, p. 16, #2.

Leo XIII: "What naturalists or rationalists aim at in philosophy, that the supporters of liberalism, carrying out the principles laid down by naturalism, are attempting in the domain of morality and politics. . . . These followers of liberalism deny the existence of any divine authority to which obedience is due, and proclaim that every man is the law to himself. So arises that ethical system which they style independent morality, and which under the guise of liberty, exonerates man from any obedience to the commands of God, and substitutes a boundless licence." *Libertas,* p. 123, #12.

30

Q. *What false principles have led to the denial of a divine origin of authority?*

A. The false principle of absolute equality of all men, the principle of sovereignty of the human reason, the principle which denies the existence of positive supernatural laws or their influence upon political life have led to a denial of the divine origin of authority.

Leo XIII: Of all the principles of naturalism "the main one lays down that as all men are alike by race and nature, so in like manner all are equal in the control of their life; that each one is so far his own master as to be in no sense under the rule of any other individual; that each is free to think on every subject just as he may choose, and to do whatever he may like to do; that no man has any right to rule over other men. In a society grounded upon such maxims, all government is nothing more nor less than the will of the people, and the people, being under the power of itself alone, is alone its own ruler. It does choose, nevertheless, some to whose charge it may commit itself, but in such wise that it makes over to them not the right so much as the business of governing, to be exercised, however, in its name. . . . And since the populace is declared to contain within itself the springhead of all rights and of all power, it follows that the State does not consider itself bound by any kind of duty towards God." *Immortale Dei,* pp. 76 and 77, #10.

LEO XIII: "The fundamental doctrine of rationalism is the supremacy of the human reason, which, refusing due submission to the divine and eternal reason, proclaims its own independence, and constitutes itself the supreme principle and source and judge of truth. . . . The end of all this can readily be foreseen, especially when society is in question. For, when once man is firmly persuaded that he is subject to no one, it follows that the efficient cause of the unity of civil society is not sought in any principle external to man, or superior to him, but simply in the free will of individuals; that the authority in the State is then taken to come from the people only; and that, just as every man's individual reason is his only rule of life, so the collective reason of the community is regarded as the supreme guide in the management of all public affairs. Hence the doctrine of the supremacy of the greatest number, and that all right and all duty reside in the majority." *Libertas* pp. 123 and 124, #12.

LEO XIII: "The first and most pernicious type of liberalism is that which on one hand rejects and destroys completely all authority and every divine law both natural and supernatural, while on the other it holds that the constitution of society is dependent upon the will of the individual and that the supreme power flows from the people as from its primary source. Then, comes the system which does recognize the natural law of God and even admits its necessity, but absolutely rejects all supernatural positive law. . . . Ultimately, there are the followers of a third type of liberalism who declare that both the life and the conduct of the individual are subject to divine laws, but these laws must exercise no influence upon the government." *Letter to the Archbishop of Bogotá.*

31

Q. *What social dangers arise from the denial of a divine origin of authority?*

A. By the denial of a divine origin of authority, the unstable whim of the majority, the will of the more aggressive group or the interests of the group in power, becomes the norm of authority. Thus, all gauge of the good and the just being lost, anything that suits one's inclination becomes licit, and the way is opened to every sort of tyranny by the strong and the shrewd.

LEO XIII: "A supreme authority which is derived from the will of the masses rather than from God, supreme, eternal and omnipotent principle of all things, loses its most august character and degenerates into an artificial sovereignty, having as its basis the unstable and changeable will of the people. Who can fail to see such consequences in modern laws? Too often, in fact, these laws express the abuse of power by the mass and the dominating will of one political party." *Giunti al venticinquesimo anno.*

LEO XIII: "Once ascribe to human reason the only authority to decide what is true and what is good, and the real distinction between good and evil is destroyed; honour and dishonour then differ, not in their nature, but in the opinion and judgment of each one; pleasure is the measure of what is lawful; and, given a code of morality which can have little or no power to restrain or quiet the unruly propensities of man, a way is naturally opened to universal corruption. With reference also to public affairs: authority is severed from the true and natural principle whence it derives all its efficacy for the common good; and the law determining what it is right to do and avoid doing is at the mercy of a majority. Now this is simply a road leading straight to tyranny. The empire of God over man and over civil society once repudiated, it follows that religion, as a public institution, can have no claim to exist, and that everything that belongs to religion will be treated with complete indifference." *Libertas,* pp. 124 and 125, #12.

32

Q. *What benefits arise from the doctrine of the divine origin of authority?*

A. Once the divine origin of authority is admitted, the right to govern becomes a legitimate function of the one invested with authority, while others have a duty to obey him. The power of governing, however, must be exercised according to truth and justice, without destroying at any time the freedom of any one of the subjects. Authority as derived from God, must function within the limits of natural and divine positive laws, as a supreme guarantee of justice and truth, the common good and the personal rights of the individual.

LEO XIII: "With regard to reconciling liberty with authority—two things which are very much confused in theory and extremely far apart in practice—Christian teachings are of immense benefit. First of all, if everyone accepts the thesis that in any form of government whatsoever the authority is derived from God, it follows that someone must have the legitimate right to rule while others have the duty to obey. Nor is this against man's dignity; because it is God to whom obedience is given even more than to man, God will hold to a much graver account those who do not represent His authority according to law and justice. On the other hand, the liberty of each individual cannot ever be suspected or abused. In order to avoid doing injustice to anyone, such liberty must be in accord with truth and justice: these are necessary requirements for public order." *Praeclara gratulationis.*

33

Q. *Is the doctrine of the divine origin of authority contrary to the human designation of the one invested with authority?*

A. To say that authority comes from God does not mean that God ordinarily designates the person who is to be invested with authority. Normally, he is designated by the community, according to methods differing from time to time and from place to place.

Leo XIII: "Those who may be placed over the State may in certain cases be chosen by the will and decision of the multitude, without opposition to or impugning of the Catholic doctrine. And by this choice, in truth, the ruler is designated, but the rights of ruling are not thereby conferred. Nor is the authority delegated to him, but the person by whom it is to be exercised is determined upon." *Diuturnum*, p. 51, #4.

Leo XIII: "There is no question here respecting forms of government, for there is no reason why the Church should not approve of the chief power being held by one man or by more, provided only it be just, and that it tend to the common advantage. Wherefore, so long as justice be respected, the people are not hindered from choosing for themselves that form of government which suits best either their own disposition, or the institutions and customs of their ancestors." *Diuturnum*, p. 51, #4.

34

Q. *What is the purpose of authority?*

A. Authority exists in order that the common good

and the good of the individual members of society may be more easily and perfectly obtained.

LEO XIII: "Those who rule states should understand that political power was not created for the advantage of any private individual; and that the administration of the State must be carried on to the profit of those who have been committed to their care, not to the profit of those to whom it has been committed." *Diuturnum*, p. 55, #12.

35

Q. *How is the authority derived from God to be exercised?*

A. Authority derived from God must be exercised with justice and fatherliness, and to the advantage of all the members of society.

LEO XIII: God "has always willed that there should be a ruling authority, and that they who are invested with it should in some measure reflect the divine power and providence over the human race. They, therefore, who rule should rule with even-handed justice, not as masters, but rather as fathers. For the rule of God over man is most just, and is tempered always with a father's kindness. Government should moreover be administered for the well-being of the citizens, because they who govern others possess authority solely for the welfare of the State. Furthermore, the civil power must not be subservient to the advantage of any one individual, or of some few persons, inasmuch as it was established for the common good of all." *Immortale Dei*, p. 67, #2.

36

Q. *What is the foundation of human laws and whence do they derive their binding force?*

A. Authority is the foundation of human law, which, if it contains precepts of natural law, derives its binding force from the eternal law.

LEO XIII: "For, since the force of law consists in the imposing of obligations and the granting of rights, authority is the one and only foundation of all law—the power, that is, of fixing duties and defining rights, as also of assigning the necessary sanctions of reward and chastisement to each and all of its commands. But all this, clearly, cannot be found in man, if, as his own supreme legislator, he is to be the rule of his actions. It follows therefore that the law of nature is the same thing as the *eternal law*, implanted in rational creatures, and inclining them to their right action and end; and can be nothing else but the eternal reason of God, the Creator and Ruler of all the world." *Libertas*, p. 119, #6.

LEO XIII: "For, what reason and the natural law do for individuals, that *human law*, promulgated for their good, does for the citizens of states. Of the laws enacted by men, some are concerned with what is good or bad by its very nature. They command men to follow after what is right and to shun what is wrong, adding at the same time a suitable sanction. But such laws by no means derive their origin from civil society; because, just as civil society did not create human nature, so neither can it be said to be the author of the good which befits human nature, or of the evil which is contrary to it. Laws come before men live together in society, and have their origin in the natural, and consequently in the eternal law. The precepts, therefore, of the natural law contained bodily in the laws of men have not merely the force of human law, but they possess that higher and more august sanction which belongs to the law of nature and the eternal law." *Libertas*, p. 120, #7.

Q. *Is authority deserving of respect and obedience?*

A. Legitimate authority must be respected and obeyed not in a half-hearted way but conscientiously.

LEO XIII: "Whence it will behoove citizens to submit themselves and to be obedient to rulers, as to God, not for their majesty; nor for the sake of pleasing, but through conscience, as doing their duty." *Diuturnum,* p. 54, #9.

LEO XIII: "To despise legitimate authority, in whomsoever vested, is unlawful, being a rebellion against the divine Will; and whoever resists such authority rushes wilfully to destruction." *Immortale Dei,* p. 68, #2.

LEO XIII: "The law of nature, no less than that of Christ, enjoins respect for all such as in their several degrees hold office in the State, and further enjoins obedience to their lawful commands. This is the only attitude worthy of a man and a Christian, and ought to be accepted heartily and as a matter of duty, 'for conscience' sake.'" *Graves de communi,* p. 233, #8.

Q. *Is disobedience to authority ever permitted?*

A. If the authority commands a thing contrary to the natural or divine positive laws, then there arises a duty not to obey it, for authority without justice is null and void.

LEO XIII: "The only reason which men have for not obeying is when anything is demanded of them which is openly repugnant to the natural or the divine law, for it is equally unlawful to command and to do anything in which the law of nature or the will of God is violated. . . . And yet there is no reason why those who so behave themselves should be accused of refusing obedience; for if the will of rulers is opposed to the will and the laws of God, they themselves exceed the bounds of their own power and pervert justice; nor can their authority then be valid, which, when there is no justice, is null." *Diuturnum*, p. 55, #11.

39

Q. *Is insurrection against authority permissible?*

A. It is not permissible to rebel unjustly against a lawfully constituted authority. However, if by unjust and other dishonest acts the one in power destroys the very foundation of authority and leads society to ruin, then it is permissible with honest and appropriate means to defend society and oneself against injustice, taking care that no greater harm is caused than was intended to be avoided.

Leo XIII: "And if at any time it happens that the power of the state is rashly and tyrannically wielded by princes, the teaching of the Catholic Church does not allow an insurrection on private authority against them, lest public order be only the more disturbed, and lest society take greater hurt therefrom. And when affairs come to such a pass that there is no other hope of safety, she teaches that relief may be hastened by the merits of Christian patience and by earnest prayers to God. But if the will of legislators and princes shall have sanctioned or commanded anything repugnant to the divine or natural law, the dignity and duty of the Christian name, as well as the judgment of the Apostle, urge that

'God is to be obeyed rather than man.'" *Quod Apostolici muneris*, p. 19, #7.

Pius XI: "The Church . . . condemns every unjust insurrection or violence against constituted powers. On the other hand, . . . whenever these powers arise against justice and truth even to destroying the very foundations of authority, it is not to be seen how those citizens are to be condemned who unite to defend themselves and the nation, by licit and appropriate means, against those who make use of public power to bring it to ruin. If the practical solution depends on concrete circumstances, we must however on our part recall to you some general principles, always to be kept in mind, and they are: 1) That these revindications have reason of means, or of relative end, not of ultimate and absolute end; 2) that as means to an end, they must be licit actions and not intrinsically evil; 3) that if they are to be means proportionate to the end, they must be used only in the measure in which they serve to obtain or render possible in whole or in part, the end, and in such manner that they do not cause to the community greater damages than those they seek to repair; 4) that the use of such means and the exercise of civic and political rights in their fullness, embracing also problems of a purely material and technical order, or any violent defense, does not enter in any such manner within the competency of the clergy or of Catholic Action as such." *Nos es muy conocida*.

Part Two

The Family Society

Chapter IV.   *The Family Society*

The Family Society

<hr />

40

Q. *What is the family?*

A. The family is a small but real society, born out of the love of a man and a woman, for the procreation and the rearing of children. Willed and ordained by God, it has its own authority and its own rights, though it reaches its natural perfection only as part of civil society.

LEO XIII: "The family . . . is a true society, governed by a power within itself, that is to say, by the father. Wherefore, provided the limits be not transgressed which are prescribed by the very purposes for which it exists, the family has, at least, equal rights with the State in the choice and pursuit of those things which are needful to its preservation and its just liberty. We say at least equal rights; for since the domestic household is anterior both in idea and in fact to the gathering of men into a commonwealth, the former must necessarily have rights and duties which are prior to those of the latter and which rest more immediately on nature." *Rerum novarum*, p. 174, #10.

LEO XIII: "The foundation of this society rests first of all on the indissoluble union of man and wife, according to the necessity of natural law, and is completed in the mutual rights and duties of parents and children." *Quod apostolici muneris*, p. 20, #8.

Pius XI: "The family is an imperfect society, since it has not in itself all the means for its own development. . . . [It] finds its own suitable temporal perfection precisely in civil society." *Divini illius magistri.*

41

Q. *What eternal laws govern the family?*

A. Natural law, given by God, and divine positive law revealed by Jesus Christ, govern completely the constitution and the essential life of the family society and no human convention, not even of the consorts themselves, can change them.

Pius XI: "Matrimony was not instituted or restored by man, but by God. Not by man were the laws made to strengthen and confirm and elevate it, but by God, the Author of nature, and by Christ our Lord, by whom nature was redeemed." *Casti connubii,* p. 126, #5.

Pius XI: The divine laws which regulate marriage "cannot be subject to any human decrees or to any contrary pact even of the spouses themselves. . . . For each individual marriage . . . arises only from the free consent of each of the spouses. . . .This freedom, however, regards only the question whether the contracting parties really wish to enter upon matrimony or to marry this particular person. The nature itself of matrimony is entirely independent of the free will of man, so that once a person has contracted matrimony he is thereby subject to its divinely made laws and its essential properties." *Casti connubii,* pp. 126 and 127, #5 and #6.

42

Q. *How is the family constituted among Catholics?*

A. Among Catholics the family is constituted by

means of matrimony, namely, "the sacrament which unites a man and a woman indissolubly and gives them the grace to live in a saintly manner and to educate their children in a Christian way." The contract cannot be separated from the sacrament.

Leo XIII: "Marriage, however, is a sacrament, because it is a holy sign which gives grace, showing forth an image of the mystical nuptials of Christ with the Church. But the form and image of these nuptials is shown precisely by the very bond of that most close union in which man and woman are bound together in one; which bond is nothing else but the marriage itself." *Arcanum*, p. 35, #12.

Leo XIII: "Certain it is that in Christian marriage the contract is inseparable from the sacrament; and that for this reason, the contract cannot be true and legitimate without being a sacrament as well. For Christ our Lord added to marriage the dignity of a sacrament; but marriage is the contract itself, whenever that contract is lawfully concluded . . . and that nothing can be further from the truth than to say that the sacrament is a certain added ornament, or outward endowment, which can be separated and torn away from the contract at the caprice of man." *Arcanum*, pp. 35 and 36, #12.

43

Q. *What are the ends of matrimony?*

A. Offspring, conjugal fidelity and the sacrament constitute the principal blessings of matrimony. Secondary ends are mutual aid, mutual love and the quieting of concupiscence.

Pius XI: " 'These,' says St. Augustine, 'are all the blessings of matrimony on account of which matrimony itself is a blessing; offspring, conjugal faith and the sacrament.'" *Casti connubii*, p. 128, #11.

LEO XIII: "Not only, in strict truth, was marriage instituted for the propagation of the human race, but also that the lives of husbands and wives might be made better and happier . . . by their lightening each others' burdens through mutual help; by constant and faithful love; by having all their possessions in common; and by the heavenly grace which flows from the sacrament. Marriage also can do much for the good of families; for, so long as it is conformable to nature and in accordance with the counsels of God, it has power to strengthen union of heart in the parents; to secure the holy education of children; to attemper the authority of the father by the example of the divine authority; to render children obedient to their parents. . . . From such marriages as these the State may rightly expect a race of citizens animated by a good spirit and filled with reverence and love for God, recognizing it as their duty to obey those who rule justly and lawfully, to love all, and to injure no one." *Arcanum*, p. 37, #14.

PIUS XI: "For in matrimony as well as in the use of the matrimonial rights there are also secondary ends, such as mutual aid, the cultivating of mutual love, and the quieting of concupiscence which husband and wife are not forbidden to consider so long as these are subordinated to the primary end and so long as the intrinsic nature of the act is preserved." *Casti connubii*, p. 145, #60.

PIUS XI: "Since, therefore, the conjugal act is destined primarily by nature for the begetting of children, those who in exercising it deliberately frustrate its natural power and purpose sin against nature and commit a deed which is shameful and intrinsically vicious." *Casti connubii*, p. 143, #55

PIUS XI: "The Catholic Church . . . raises her voice. . . :

any use whatsoever of matrimony exercised in such a way that the act is deliberately frustrated in its natural power to generate life is an offense against the law of God and of nature, and those who indulge in such are branded with the guilt of a grave sin." *Casti connubii,* p. 144, #57.

44

Q. *Is there among Christians a matrimony which is not a sacramental union?*

A. A non-sacramental union of a Christian man and woman, even if it conforms to civil laws, cannot be considered to be more than a mere rite introduced by civil law.

Leo XIII: "Now, those who deny that marriage is holy, and who relegate it, stripped of all sacredness, to the class of common things, uproot thereby the foundations of nature. They not only resist the designs of Providence, but, so far as they can, they destroy the order that God has ordained." *Arcanum,* p. 36, #13.

Leo XIII: "If there be any union of a man and woman among the faithful of Christ which is not a sacrament, such union has not the force and nature of a proper marriage; and, although contracted in accordance with the laws of the State, it cannot be more than a rite or custom introduced by the civil law." *Arcanum,* pp. 44 and 45, #25.

45

Q. *What are the properties of matrimony?*

A. Unity and indissolubility are the properties of Christian matrimony.

Pius XI: "Conjugal faith . . . demands in the first place

the complete unity of matrimony. . . . There is no doubt that the law of the Gospel fully restored that original and perfect unity, and abrogated all dispensations." *Casti connubii,* p. 132, #20.

Pius XI: "But this accumulation of benefits is completed and, as it were, crowned by that blessing of Christian marriage which in the words of St. Augustine we have called the sacrament, by which is denoted both the indissolubility of the bond and the raising and hallowing of the contract by Christ Himself, whereby He made it an efficacious sign of grace." *Casti connubii,* p. 135, #31.

Pius XI: "And if this stability seems to be open to exception, however rare the exception may be, as in the case of certain natural marriages between unbelievers, or among Christians in the case of those marriages which though valid have not been consummated, that exception does not depend on the will of men nor on that of any merely human power, but on divine law, of which the only guardian and interpreter is the Church of Christ. However, not even this power can ever affect for any cause whatsoever a Christian marriage which is valid and has been consummated." *Casti connubii, p.* 136, #35.

Leo XIII: "Jesus Christ bore witness to the Jews and to His Apostles that marriage, from its institution, should exist between two only, namely, between one man and one woman; that of two they are made, so to say, one flesh; and that the marriage bond is by the will of God so closely and strongly made fast that no man may dissolve it or rend it asunder. 'For this cause shall a man leave father and mother, and shall cleave to his wife, and they two shall be in one flesh. Therefore now they are not two, but one flesh. What, therefore, God hath joined together, let no man put asunder' (Matt. 19: 5–6)." *Arcanum* p. 27, #4.

Q. *To whom is the discipline concerning matrimony
reserved?*

A. Since matrimony is by its own nature a sacred
thing and a sacrament by the will of Christ, its
discipline belongs to the Church, who freely
and constantly has exercised it down through
the centuries.

Leo XIII: This pope sustains that matrimonial discipline is reserved to the Church: "1) Since marriage,
then, is holy by its own power, in its own nature, and
of itself, it ought not to be regulated and administered
by the will of civil rulers, but by the divine authority of
the Church, which alone in sacred matters professes the
office of teaching. 2) But to decree and ordain concerning the sacrament is, by the will of Christ Himself,
the duty of the Church alone. 3) Lastly must be borne
in mind the great weight and crucial test of history, by
which it is plainly proved that the legislative and
judicial authority of which we are speaking has been
freely and constantly used by the Church, even in times
when some foolishly suppose the head of the State
either to have consented to it or connived at it." *Arcanum*, pp. 33 and 34, #11.

Q. *Who regulates the civil effects of matrimony?*

A. Since there are civil effects that flow from matrimony and since matrimony has relationships
with human elements belonging to the civil
order of things, such effects and relationships
are legitimately regulated by the State.

LEO XIII: The Church "is not unaware and never calls in doubt, that the sacrament of marriage, since it was instituted for the preservation and increase of the human race, has a necessary relation to various circumstances of life, which, though connected with marriage, belong to the civil order, and about which the State rightly makes strict enquiry and justly promulgates decrees." *Arcanum*, p. 42, #21.

LEO XIII: "The civil law can deal with and decide those matters alone which in the civil order spring from marriage." *Arcanum* p. 44, #25.

48

Q. *What fallacies exist today with regard to marriage?*

A. Erroneously it is said that matrimony is a human invention to be governed only by civil regulations, which can dissolve marriages just as they sanction them. Others add that it is not a duty of the State to protect conjugal fidelity and that it must facilitate the social, economic, and physiological emancipation of the woman. Others hold that it should be permissible for parents to suppress offspring yet unborn, according to their whim. Others hold that for the protection of the race civil authority can forbid defective people from entering marriage even to the point of making them sterile, despite their unwillingness.

PIUS XI: Error #1: " . . . that matrimony is repeatedly declared to be not instituted by the Author of nature nor raised by Christ the Lord to the dignity of a true sacrament, but invented by man."

Error #2: "Some confidently assert that they have found

no evidence for the existence of matrimony in nature or in her laws, but regard it merely as the means of producing life and of gratifying in one way or another a vehement impulse."

Error #3. "On the other hand, others recognize that certain beginnings or, as it were, seeds of true wedlock are found. . . . At the same time they maintain that in all beyond this germinal idea matrimony, through various concurrent causes, is invented solely by the mind of man, established solely by his will." *Casti connubii*, pp. 141 and 142, #50.

Pius XI: "They put forward in the first place that matrimony belongs entirely to the profane and purely civil sphere, that it is not to be committed to the religious society, the Church of Christ, but to civil society alone. They then add that the marriage contract is to be freed from any indissoluble bond, and that separation and divorce are not only to be tolerated but sanctioned by the law. (#80) The first point is contained in their contention that the civil act itself should stand for the marriage contract (civil matrimony, as it is called), while the religious act is to be considered a mere addition. (#81) Moreover they want it to be no cause for reproach that marriages be contracted by Catholics with non-Catholics without any reference to religion or recourse to the ecclesiastical authorities. The second point, which is but a consequence of the first, is to be found in their excuse for complete divorce and in their praise and encouragement of those civil laws which favor the loosening of the bond itself." *Casti connubii*, p. 152, #80 and #81.

Pius XI: "They look upon whatever penal laws are passed by the State for the preserving of conjugal faith as void or to be abolished. Such unworthy and idle opinions are condemned by that noble instinct which is found in every chaste husband and wife, and even by the light of the testimony of nature alone—a testimony that is sanctioned and confirmed by the command of God: 'Thou shalt not commit adultery' (Exod. 20:14), and the words of Christ: 'Anyone who even looks with lust at a woman has already committed adultery with her in his heart." (Matt. 5:28). . . . The same false teachers . . . do not scruple to do away with the honorable and trusting obedience which the woman owes to the man. Many of them even go further and assert . . . that the rights of husband and wife are equal; wherefore, they boldly proclaim, the emancipation of women has been or ought to be effected. . . . It must be social, economic, physiological. . . . This equality of rights . . . must indeed be recognized in those rights which belong to the dignity of the human soul and which are proper to the marriage contract and inseparably bound up with wedlock." *Casti connubii,* pp. 150 and 151, #73, 74, 75, 76.

Pius XI: "But another very grave crime is to be noted . . . which regards the taking of the life of the off-spring hidden in the mother's womb. Some wish it to be allowed and left to the will of the father or the mother; others say it is unlawful unless there are weighty reasons which they call by the name of medical, social, or eugenic 'indication.' Because this matter falls under the penal laws of the State by which the destruction of the off-spring begotten but unborn is forbidden, these people demand that the 'indication,' which in one form or another they defend, be recognized as such by the public law and in no way penalized. There are those, moreover, who ask that the public authorities provide aid for these death-dealing operations. . . . As to the 'medical and therapeutic indication,' nevertheless, what could ever be a sufficient reason for excusing in any way the direct murder of the innocent? . . . Whether inflicted upon the mother or upon the child, it is against the precept of God and the law of nature: 'Thou shalt not kill.' . . . What is asserted in favor of the social and eugenic 'indication' may and must be accepted, provided lawful and upright methods are employed within the proper limits; but to wish to put forward reasons based upon them for the killing of the innocent is unthinkable and contrary to the divine precept promulgated in the words of the Apostle: 'Evil is not to be done that good may come of it' (Rom. 3:8)." *Casti connubii,* pp. 146 and 147, #63, 64, 66.

Pius XI: "For there are some who, oversolicitous for the cause of 'eugenics' . . . put 'eugenics' before aims of a higher order. By public authority they wish to forbid marriage to all those who, even though naturally fit for marriage, are regarded, in accordance with the norms and conjectures of their investigations, as persons who through hereditary transmission would bring forth defective offspring. And, more, they wish to legislate to deprive these of that natural faculty by medical action, despite their unwillingness. And this they propose to do, not as an infliction of grave punishment under the authority of the State for a crime committed, nor to prevent future crimes by guilty persons; but against every right and good they wish the civil authority to arrogate to itself a power over a faculty which it never had and never can legitimately possess. Those who act in this way are at fault in losing sight of the fact that the family is more sacred than the State and that men are begotten not for the earth and for time, but for heaven and eternity. Although often these individuals are to be dissuaded from entering into matrimony, certainly it is wrong to brand men with the stigma of crime because they contract marriage, on the ground that, despite the fact that they are in every respect capable of matrimony, they will give birth only to defective children, even though they use all care and diligence." *Casti connubii,* p. 148, #68 and 69.

Pius XI: The errors on matrimony are "plainly seen

from the consequences which its advocates deduce from it, namely, that the laws, institutions, and customs by which wedlock is governed, since they take their origin solely from the will of man, are subject entirely to him, hence can and must be founded, changed, and abrogated according to human caprice and the shifting circumstances of human affairs; that the generative power which is grounded in nature itself is more sacred and has wider range than matrimony—hence it may be exercised both outside as well as within the confines of wedlock, even though the purpose of matrimony be set aside, as though to suggest that the licence of a base fornicating woman should enjoy the same rights as the chaste motherhood of a lawfully wedded wife.

"Armed with these principles, some men go so far as to concoct new species of unions, suited, as they say, to the present temper of men and the times, which various new forms of matrimony they presume to label 'temporary,' 'experimental,' and 'companionate.' These offer all the indulgence of matrimony and its rights without, however, the indissoluble bond, and without offspring, unless later the parties alter their cohabitation into a matrimony in the full sense of the law.

"Indeed there are some who desire and insist that these practices be legalized by the law, or, at least, excused by their general acceptance among the people. They do not seem even to suspect that these proposals partake of nothing of the modern 'culture' in which they glory so much, but are simply hateful abominations which beyond all question reduce our truly cultured nations to the barbarous standards of savage peoples." *Casti connubii*, pp. 142 and 143, #51, 52 and 53.

49

Q. *Is the separation of consorts permissible?*

A. For grave reasons, and when all other remedies

have failed, the separation of consorts is allowed.

Leo XIII: "When, indeed, matters have come to such a pitch that it seems impossible for them to live together any longer, then the Church allows them to live apart, and strives at the same time to soften the evils of this separation by such remedies and helps as are suited to their condition; yet she never ceases to endeavor to bring about a reconciliation, and never despairs of doing so." *Arcanum*, p. 44, #25.

50

Q. *Can a true marriage be dissolved?*

A. Since the marriage bond is by its very nature indissoluble, no authority in the world can dissolve it, if the marriage is ratified and consummated. The annulments, improperly so-called, are verifications, based on certain proofs, of the non-existence of the bond.

Leo XIII: " . . . that no power can dissolve the bond of Christian marriage whenever this has been ratified and consummated." *Arcanum*, p. 44, #25.

51

Q. *What evil effects are produced by divorce?*

A. Divorce favors inconsiderate unions, renders marriage unstable, encourages infidelity, weakens parental authority, perverts morals, brings damage to the well-being and the rearing of offspring, leads entire nations to ruin.

Leo XIII: "Matrimonial contracts are by it made variable, mutual kindness is weakened, deplorable inducements to unfaithfulness are supplied, harm is done to the education and training of children, occasion is afforded for the breaking up of homes, the seeds of dissension are sown among families, the dignity of womanhood is lessened and brought low, and women run the risk of being deserted after having ministered to the pleasures of men. Since, then, nothing has such power to lay waste families and destroy the mainstay of kingdoms as the corruption of morals, it is easily seen that divorces are in the highest degree hostile to the prosperity of families and states, springing as they do from the depraved morals of the people, and, as experience shows us, opening out a way to every kind of evil-doing in public as well as in private life." *Arcanum*, p. 39, #17.

LEO XIII: "When the stability which is imparted to it by religious wedlock is lost, it follows that the power of the father over his own children, and the duties of the children toward their parents, must be greatly weakened." *Quod apostolici muneris,* p. 20, #8.

52

Q. *What are the benefits that flow from the indissolubility of matrimony?*

A. The indissolubility of matrimony confers great security to the consorts, infidelity is contained, mutual help enhanced, the care and the education of children is favored, morals are protected, society is placed on the path of tranquillity and order.

PIUS XI: Advantages derived from the indissolubility of marriage are: "First of all, both husband and wife possess a positive guarantee of the endurance of this stability which assures that generous yielding of their persons and the intimate fellowship of their hearts. . . . Besides, a strong bulwark is set up in defense of a loyal chastity against incitements to infidelity, should any be encountered either from within or from without. Any anxious fear lest in adversity or old age the other spouse would prove unfaithful is precluded and in its place there reigns a calm sense of security. Moreover, the dignity of both man and wife is maintained and mutual aid is most satisfactorily assured. . . . In the training and education of children . . . it plays a great part. . . . For experience has taught that unassailable stability in matrimony is a fruitful source of virtuous life and of habits of integrity. Where this order of things obtains, the happiness and well-being of the nation is safely guarded." *Casti connubii,* pp. 137 and 138, #37.

53

Q. *What are the guarantees for the well-being of the family?*

A. The family will obtain a full measure of well-being if set up according to Christian principles; it shall receive all possible aids from religion, shall be cemented by the love of parents, prudently directed by the authority of the father, and shall by the free exercise of its rights attend to the education of offspring.

LEO XIII: "If the family is governed by the rules of Christian life, each member of it will gradually become accustomed to cherish religion and piety, to reject with horror all false and pernicious doctrines, to practice virtue, to render obedience to the authorities, and to repress the insatiable egotism which so greatly debases and enfeebles human nature." *Inscrutabili Dei consilio,* p. 11, #15.

LEO XIII: "They [husband and wife] are bound, namely, to have such feelings for one another as to cherish always very great mutual love, to be ever faithful to their marriage vow, and to give to one another an unfailing and unselfish help. The husband is the chief of the family, and the head of the wife . . . [who] must be subject to her husband and obey him; not, indeed, as a servant, but as a companion, so that her obedience shall be wanting in neither honour nor dignity . . . both in him who commands and in her who obeys, a heaven-born love guiding both in their respective duties." *Arcanum,* p. 30, #8.

PIUS XI: "The family therefore holds directly from the Creator the mission and hence the right to educate the offspring, a right inalienable because inseparably joined to the strict obligation, a right anterior to any right whatever of civil society and of the State, and therefore inviolable on the part of any power on earth." *Divini illius magistri.*

54

Q. *To achieve its perfection, does the family need to be integrated in civil society or the State?*

A. The inadequacy of the means necessary for the family to reach its ends, makes the integrating action by the State useful and sometimes absolutely indispensable. This action, however, must be contained within the limits of the well-being of the family itself and must enhance, rather than infringe upon, the rights of the family or diminish its possibilities.

LEO XIII: "Wherefore, provided the limits be not transgressed which are prescribed by the very purposes for which it exists, the family has, at least, equal rights with the State in the choice and pursuit of those things which are needful to its preservation and its just liberty. We say, at least equal rights; for since the domestic household is anterior both in idea and in fact to the gathering of men into a commonwealth, the former must necessarily have rights and duties which are prior to those of the latter, and which rest more immediately on nature. If the citizens of a State, if the families, on entering into association and fellowship, experienced at the hands of the State hindrance instead of help, and found their rights attacked instead of being protected, such association were rather to be repudiated than sought after. The idea, then, that the civil government should, at its own discretion, penetrate and pervade the family and the household, is a great and pernicious mistake. True, if a family find itself in great difficulty, utterly friendless, and without prospect of help, it is right that extreme necessity be met by public aid. . . . In like manner, if within the walls of the household there occur a grave disturbance of mutual rights, the public power must intervene to force each party to give the other what is due. . . . But the rulers of the State must go no further: nature bids them stop here. Paternal authority can neither be abolished by the State nor absorbed." *Rerum novarum*, p. 174, #10 and 11.

Pius XI: "Now, since it is no rare thing to find that the peculiar purpose, the generation and formation of offspring . . . has priority of nature and therefore of rights over civil society. Nevertheless, the family is an imperfect society, since it has not in itself all the means for its own complete development . . . [but] finds its own suitable temporal perfection precisely in civil society." *Divini illius magistri.*

Pius XI: "Now, since it is no rare thing to find that the perfect observance of God's commands and conjugal integrity encounters difficulties because husband and wife are in straitened circumstances, their necessities must be relieved as far as possible. And so, in the first place, every effort should be made . . . namely, that in the state such economic and social methods should be adopted as will enable every head of a family to earn as much as, according to his station in life, is necessary for himself, his wife, and for the rearing of his children. . . .

"Care, however, must be taken that the parties themselves, for a considerable time before entering upon married life, should strive to dispose of, or at least to diminish, the material obstacles in their way. . . . Provision must be made also, in the case of those who are not self-supporting, for joint aid by private or public guilds.

"When these means which We have pointed out do not fulfill the needs, particularly of a larger or poorer family, Christian charity toward our neighbor absolutely demands that those things which are lacking to the needy should be provided; hence it is incumbent on the rich to help the poor, so that, having an abundance of this world's goods, they may not expend them fruitlessly or completely squander them, but employ them for the support and well-being of those who lack the necessities of life.

"If, however, for this purpose, private resources do not suffice, it is the duty of the public authority to supply for the insufficient forces of individual effort. . . . Hence, in making the laws and in disposing of public funds they must do their utmost to relieve the needs of the poor. . . ." *Casti connubii*, p. 168, #122–126.

Part Three

The State and The Citizen

Chapter V. *Nature, Ends, and Powers of the State*

Chapter VI. *The Citizen in Public Life*

Nature, Ends, and Powers of the State

55

Q. *What is civil society or the State?*

A. The State is a society naturally formed, necessary to man's perfection, possessing all the means useful to the achievement of its end, occupying a determined area, consisting of a certain group of people, living under contingent forms of organization of the sovereign power.

Leo XIII: "Man's natural instinct moves him to live in civil society. Isolated he cannot provide himself with the necessary requirements of life, nor procure the means of developing his mental and moral faculties." *Immortale Dei,* p. 66, #2.

Pius XI: "Civil society is a perfect society, having in itself all the means for its peculiar end." *Divini illius magistri.*

Pius XII: "The State does not contain in itself and does not mechanically bring together in a given territory a shapeless mass of individuals. It is, and should in practice be, the organic and organizing unity of a real people." *Christmas Message,* 1944.

56

Q. *What is the end of the State?*

A. The State, as a necessary medium at the service of the human person, must control, help, and regulate private and individual activities of national life in order that they may tend harmoniously toward the common good.

Pius XII: "It was the Creator's will that civil sovereignty should regulate social life after the dictates of an order changeless in its universal principles; should facilitate the attainment in the temporal order, by individuals, of physical, intellectual and moral perfection; and should aid them to reach their supernatural end. Hence, it is the noble prerogative and function of the State to control, aid and direct the private and individual activities of national life that they converge harmoniously towards the common good. That good can neither be defined according to arbitrary ideas nor can it accept for its standard primarily the material prosperity of society, but rather it should be defined according to the harmonious development and the natural perfection of man. It is for this perfection that society is designed by the Creator as a means." *Summi pontificatus*, pp. 15–16, #58 and 59.

Pius XI: "Catholic doctrine indicates to the State the dignity and authority of a vigilant and provident defender of those divine and human rights. . . ." *Divini Redemptoris*, p. 353, #32.

Pius XII: "To consider the State as something ultimate to which everything else should be subordinated and directed, cannot fail to harm the true and lasting prosperity of nations." *Summi pontificatus*, p. 16, #60.

57

Q. *What is the common good to be attained by the State?*

A. The common good to be attained by the State, or the common temporal good, consists in the peaceful and safe enjoyment by all citizens of their own rights, and in the maximum attainable material and spiritual welfare, in accordance with the times and the possibilities.

Pius XI: "The common welfare in the temporal order, consists in that peace and security in which families and individual citizens have the free exercise of their rights, and at the same time enjoy the greatest spiritual and temporal prosperity possible in this life, by the mutual union and coordination of the work of all." *Divini illius magistri.*

58

Q. *Within what limits must the State operate so that the common good may be attained?*

A. The State must respect the natural rights of the person (Cf. Chapter I, art. 1) and those of the other necessary societies, and integrate, without suppressing them, all other minor societies and private initiatives favoring the perfecting of the human person. Otherwise, the common good cannot be attained.

Pius XII: "And when it disregards the respect due to the human person and to the life which is proper to that person, and gives no thought to it in its organization, in legislative and executive activity, then instead of serving society, it harms it; instead of encouraging and stimulating social thought, instead of realizing its hopes and expectations, it strips it of all real value." *Christmas Message,* 1942.

Leo XIII: "We have said that the State must not absorb

the individual or the family; both should be allowed free and untrammeled action as far as is consistent with the common good and the interests of others." *Rerum novarum*, pp. 187–188, #28.

Pius XII: If, in fact, the State lays claim to and directs private enterprises, these, ruled as they are by delicate and complicated internal principles which guarantee and assure the realization of their special aims, may be damaged to the detriment of the public good, by being wrenched from their natural surroundings, that is, from responsible private action." *Summi pontificatus*, p. 16, #60.

Pius XII: "The purpose of the whole of the State's activity, political and economic, is the permanent realization of the common good; that is to say, the provision of those external conditions which are needful to citizens as a whole for the development of their qualities and the fulfillment of their duties in every sphere of life, material, intellectual, and religious—in the supposition, however, that the powers and energies of the family and of other organisms which hold natural precedence over the State are insufficient, and also subject to the fact that God, in His will for the salvation of men, has instituted another universal society, the Church, for the benefit of the human person and for the realization of his religious ends." *Christmas Message*, 1942.

Pius XII: "The citizens must not be compelled without being heard." *Christmas Message*, 1944.

Pius XII: "In some countries the modern State is becoming a gigantic administrative machine. It extends its influence over almost every phase of life; it would bring under its administration the entire gamut of political, economic, social and intellectual life from birth to death. No wonder then if, in this impersonal atmosphere, which tends to penetrate and pervade all human life, respect for the common good becomes dormant in the conscience of individuals and the State loses more and more its primary character of a community of morally responsible citizens." *Christmas Message,* 1952.

59

Q. *Does the State have an educational mission?*

A. The State must favor and integrate the educational mission of family and Church and fulfill its own mission promoting the civic, cultural, physical, administrative and military education necessary to all or to certain categories of citizens so that the common good may be attained.

Pius XI: "The true and just rights of the State in regard to the education of its citizens . . . have been conferred upon civil society by the Author of nature Himself, not by the title of fatherhood, as in the case of the Church and of the family, but in virtue of the authority which it possesses to promote the common temporal welfare, which is precisely the purpose of its existence. Consequently education cannot pertain to civil society in the same way in which it pertains to the Church and to the family, but in a different way corresponding to its own particular end. . . . The function therefore of the civil authority residing in the State is twofold, to protect and to foster, but by no means to absorb, the family and the individual, or to substitute itself for them. Accordingly in the matter of education, it is the right, or, to speak more correctly, it is the duty of the State to protect in its legislation, the prior rights of the family . . . and consequently also to respect the supernatural rights of the Church. . . . It also belongs to the State to protect the rights of the child itself. . . . In general, then, it is the right and duty of the State to protect, according to the rules of right reason and faith, the moral and religious education of youth, by removing public impediments that stand in the way. In the first place it pertains to the State, in view of the common good, to promote in various ways the education and instruction of youth. It should begin by encouraging and assisting, of its own accord, the initiative and activity of the Church and the family. . . . It should, moreover, supplement their work whenever this falls short of what is necessary, even by means of its own schools and institutions. . . . Over and above this, the State can exact and take measures to secure that all its citizens have the necessary knowledge of their civic and political duties, and a certain degree of physical, intellectual and moral culture, which, considering the conditions of our times, is really necessary for the common good. However, it is clear that in all these ways of promoting education and instruction, both public and private, the State should respect the inherent rights of the Church and of the family. . . . This does not prevent the State from reserving to itself the establishment and direction of schools intended to prepare for certain civic duties and especially for military service. . . . In general also it belongs to civil society and the State to provide what may be called civic education, not only for its youth, but for all ages and classes. This consists in the practice of presenting publicly to groups of individuals information having an intellectual imaginative and emotional appeal, calculated to draw their wills to what is upright and honest, and to urge its practice by a sort of moral compulsion, positively by disseminating such knowledge, and negatively by suppressing what is opposed to it. This civic education, so wide and varied in itself as to include almost every activity of the State intended for the public good, ought also to be regulated by the norms of rectitude, and therefore cannot conflict with the doctrines of the Church, which is the divinely appointed teacher of these norms." *Divini illius magistri.*

Q. *Does the State have religious duties of its own?*

A. The State, with its own means, has the obligation to honor God in the manner which He Himself has requested through Revelation, to respect the laws and to see that they be respected, to favor the Church in the fulfillment of its mission and to help the citizens in the pursuit of their ultimate end.

LEO XIII: "Nature and reason, commanding every individual devoutly to worship God in holiness . . . bind also the civil community by a like law. For men living together in society, no less than individuals, are under the power of God; and society, no less than individuals, owes gratitude to God. . . . No one, then, is allowed to be remiss in the service due to God, while the chief duty of all men is to cling to religion in both its teaching and practice—not such religion as each may prefer, but the religion which God enjoins and which certain and most clear marks show to be the one and only true religion. . . . So, too, is it a sin in the State not to have any care for religion, as if this were something beyond its scope, or of no practical benefit; or else out of many forms of religion to adopt that one which chimes in with its fancy. For we are bound absolutely to worship God in that way which He has shown to be His will. All who rule, therefore, should hold in honour the holy Name of God. One of their chief duties must be to favour religion, to protect it, to shield it under the credit and sanction of the laws, and neither to organize nor enact any measures that may compromise its safety. This is the bounden duty of rulers to the people over whom they rule: for one and all we are destined, by our birth and adoption, to enjoy after this frail and fleeting life the supreme and final good in heaven. . . . In as far, then, as on this depends the full and perfect happiness of mankind, the securing of this end should be of all imaginable interests the most urgent. Hence civil society, established for the common welfare, should not only safeguard the well-being of the community, but should have at heart also the interests of its individual members, and that in such a manner as not to hinder, but in every way to render as easy as possible the possession of that highest and unchangeable good for which all should strive. For this purpose, care must especially be taken to preserve unharmed and unimpeded the practice of religion which is the bond connecting man with God." *Immortale Dei,* pp. 68–69, #3.

PIUS XI: "The believer has an inalienable right to profess his faith and put it into practice in the manner suited to him. Laws that suppress or make this profession and practice difficult contradict the natural law." *Mit brennender Sorge.*

PIUS XI: "All diligence should be exercised by states to prevent within their territories the ravages of an anti-God campaign which shakes society to its very foundations. For there can be no authority on earth unless the authority of the Divine Majesty be recognized; no oath will bind which is not sworn in the Name of the Living God." *Divini Redemptoris,* p. 371, #80.

LEO XIII: "To hold, therefore, that there is no difference in matters of religion between forms that are unlike each other, and even contrary to each other, most clearly leads in the end to the rejection of all religion in both theory and practice. And this is the same thing as atheism, however it may differ from it in name. Men who really believe in the existence of God must, in order to be consistent with themselves and to avoid absurd conclusions, understand that differing modes of divine worship, involving dissimilarity and conflict even on most important points, cannot all be equally probable, equally good, and equally acceptable to God." *Immortale Dei*, p. 80, #14.

LEO XIII: "It is not lawful for the State, any more than for the individual, either to disregard all religious duties, or to hold in equal favour different kinds of religion." *Immortale Dei*, p. 83, #17.

LEO XIII: "The Church, indeed, deems it unlawful to place various forms of divine worship on the same footing as the true religion, but does not, on that account, condemn those rulers who for the sake of securing some great good, or of hindering some great evil, tolerate in practice that these various forms of religion have a place in the State." *Ibid*.

61

Q. *Is the State the protector of liberty?*

A. For the triumph of truth and the respect of the human person, the State must protect full liberty in all opinionable matters; but it cannot permit without neglecting its own duties abuses contrary to truth, justice and the common good, unless such toleration is productive of greater good.

LEO XIII: "It is hardly necessary to say that there can be no such right as this [liberty of speech and liberty of the press] if it be not used in moderation, and if it pass beyond the bounds and ends of all liberty. . . . In regard, however, to any matters of opinion which God leaves to man's free discussion, full liberty of thought and of speech is naturally within the right of everyone; for such liberty never leads men to suppress the truth, but often to discover it and make it known." *Libertas*, pp. 128, 130, #18.

LEO XIII: "Liberty is a power perfecting man, and

hence should have truth and goodness for its object. . . . Whatever, therefore, is opposed to virtue and truth, may not rightly be brought temptingly before the eye of man, much less sanctioned by the favour and protection of the law . . . and on this account the State is acting against the laws and dictates of nature whenever it permits the licence of opinion and of action to lead minds astray from truth, and souls away from the practice of virtue." *Libertas*, p. 80, #15.

LEO XIII: "Therefore, the true liberty of human society does not consist in every man doing what he pleases, for this would simply end in turmoil and confusion, and bring on the overthrow of the State; but rather in this, that through the injunctions of the civil law all may more easily conform to the prescriptions of the eternal law." *Libertas*, p. 121, #7.

LEO XIII: "The Church . . . while not conceding any right to anything save what is true and honest, does not forbid public authority to tolerate what is at variance with truth and justice, for the sake of avoiding some greater evil, or of obtaining or preserving some greater good. . . . But if, in such circumstances, for the sake of the common good (and this is the only legitimate reason), human law may or even should tolerate evil, it may not and should not approve or desire evil for its own sake." *Libertas*, p. 134, #23.

62

Q. *Must the State take care of the citizens' economic welfare?*

A. The State must participate in the creation of those conditions without which it is not possible for the members of the community to attain their own welfare. This it must do respecting and exacting respect for the natural rights of the person, and integrating the insufficiencies of the individuals and of minor societies.

Pius XI: "It must likewise be the special care of the State to create those material conditions of life without which an orderly society cannot exist." *Divini Redemptoris*, p. 372, #81.

Leo XIII: "The first duty, therefore, of the rulers of the State should be to make sure that the laws and institutions, the general character and administration of the commonwealth, shall be such as to produce of themselves public well-being and private prosperity. . . . Whenever the general interest of any particular class suffers, or is threatened with evils which can in no other way be met, the public authority must step in to meet them." *Rerum novarum*, p. 185, #26; p. 188, #28.

Pius XI: "If, however, for this purpose, private resources do not suffice, it is the duty of the public authority to supply for the insufficient forces of individual effort." *Casti connubii*, p. 169, #126.

Pius XI: "Just as it is wrong to take away from individuals what by their own ability and effort they can accomplish and commit it to the community, so it is an injury and at the same time both a serious evil and a perturbation of right order to assign to a larger and higher society what can be performed successfully by smaller and lower communities. . . . The state, then, should leave to these smaller groups the settlement of business and problems of minor importance, which should otherwise greatly distract it. Thus it will carry out with greater freedom, power, and success the tasks belonging to it alone, because it alone is qualified to perform them: directing, watching, stimulating, and restraining, as circumstances suggest or necessity demands." *Quadragesimo anno*, p. 207, #79 and 80.

Q. *By what means can the State procure public prosperity?*

A. By promoting good morals and order, the family, religion and justice, and a moderate and just distribution of obligations, and by favoring the development of economic activities, the State can foster public prosperity.

LEO XIII: "Now, a State chiefly prospers and flourishes by morality, by well-regulated family life, by respect for religion and justice, by the moderation and equal distribution of public burdens, by the progress of the arts and of trade, by the abundant yield of the land—by everything, in brief, whose cultivation makes the citizens better and happier. Here, then, it is in the power of a ruler to benefit every order of the State, and amongst the rest to promote in the highest degree the interests of the poor. This he will do by virtue of his office, and without being exposed to any suspicion of undue interference; for it is the province of the commonwealth to consult the common good. And the more that is done for the working population by the general laws of the country, the less need will there be to seek for particular means to relieve them." *Rerum novarum*, p. 186, #26.

64

Q. *Is there a form of government that is good for all States?*

A. Human wisdom is free to select the form of government that is more in accord with the historical necessities of each individual people, provided that the rights of the human person, the common good, the origin and the use of power are properly preserved. Today, the democratic form seems to be such.

LEO XIII: "No one of the several forms of government is in itself condemned, insofar as none of them contains anything contrary to Catholic doctrine, and all of them are capable, if wisely and justly managed, of insuring the welfare of the State." *Immortale Dei*, p. 83, #18.

LEO XIII: "But in matters merely political, as for instance the best form of government, and this or that system of administration, a difference of opinion is lawful." *Immortale Dei*, p. 89, #23.

LEO XIII: "Again, it is not of itself wrong to prefer a democratic form of government, if only the Catholic doctrine be maintained as to the origin and exercise of power. Of the various forms of government, the Church does not reject any that are fitted to procure the welfare of the subject." *Libertas*, p. 138, #32.

PIUS XII: "It is scarcely necessary to recall that according to the teaching of the Church, 'it is not forbidden to prefer temperate, popular forms of government, without prejudice, however, to Catholic teaching on the origin and use of authority.' . . . 'The Church does not disapprove of any of the various forms of government provided they be *per se* capable of securing the good of the citizens.' . . . Our action shows clearly that the interest and solicitude of the Church looks not so much to its external structure and organization, as to the individual himself who, far from being the object and, as it were, a merely passive element in the social order, is in fact, and must be and continue to be, its subject, its foundation and its end. A healthy and true democracy responding also to the social tone proper to the charity of the Church, can be realized in monarchies as well as republics." *Christmas Message*, 1944.

Q. *Under what conditions can a genuinely demo-cratic form of government satisfy present-day needs?*

A. It is possible to establish a genuinely democratic form of government according to present-day needs if: 1) the people organized in a State control its own organs and concur to the formation of the will of the community through capable representatives, endowed with high moral sense; 2) if the authority has effective power, limited only by the respect for the will of the people and by moral laws; 3) if the rulers fulfill their duties with full awareness of their high mission; 4) if all citizens have a moral maturity enlightened by the light of Christian truths.

Pius XII: "The citizens must not be compelled to obey without being heard. . . . The State is, and should in practice be, the organic and organizing unity of a real people. . . .

"The State . . . should be entrusted with the power to command with real and effective authority. . . . Only a clear appreciation of the purpose assigned by God to every human society, joined to a deep sense of the exalted duties of social activity, can put those in power in a position to fulfill their own obligations in the legislative, judicial and executive order with that objectivity impartiality, loyalty, generosity and integrity without which a democratic government would find it hard to command the respect and the support of the better section of the people. . . .

"The center of a democracy normally set up resides in

this popular assembly. . . . The question of high moral standards, practical ability and intellectual capacity of parliamentary deputies is for every people living under a democratic regime a question of life and death, of prosperity and decadence, of soundness or perpetual unrest. . . .

"A sound democracy, based on the immutable principles of the natural law and revealed truth, will resolutely turn its back on such corruption as gives to the state legislature an unchecked and unlimited power, and moreover, makes the democratic regime, notwithstanding an outward show to the contrary, purely and simply a form of absolutism.

"This form of [democratic] government makes exalted claims on the moral maturity of the individual citizen; a moral maturity to which he could never hope to attain fully and securely if the light from the Cave of Bethlehem did not illumine the dark path along which the peoples are going forward through the stormy present towards a future which they hope will be more serene." *Christmas Message,* 1944.

66

Q. *Are there any forms of government unsuited for the State, as the instrument through which the common good is attained?*

A. Forms of government based on atheism, or forms which subordinate the right of the individual to the power of the State, or which foster only the material welfare to which every other aspect of life is sacrificed or leave the common good to the outcome of a competition between various egotistic aims or to the will of a tyrant ruler are unsuited for a State conceived according to Christian principles.

Pius XI: "In the Communistic commonwealth morality and law would be nothing but a derivation of the existing economic order, purely earthly in origin and unstable in character. In a word, the Communists claim to inaugurate a new era and a new civilization which is the result of blind evolutionary forces culminating in a 'humanity without God.'" *Divini Redemptoris,* p. 346, #12.

Pius XI: It is not a prerogative of the State to be a "subjective totalitarianism in which every aspect of the life of the individual is subordinated to the State and made dependent upon the State (*a fortiori* if the citizen is made to depend exclusively or principally upon the State). This would mean that the citizen is made to depend upon the State for everything that is or could be necessary to human life, particularly to man's individual life, to the life of his family, to his spiritual and supernatural life." *Dobbiamo intrattenerla.*

Pius XI: "Socialism, on the contrary, entirely ignorant of and unconcerned about this sublime end both of individuals and of society, affirms that human society was instituted merely for the sake of material advantages. . . . The socialists argue that economic production . . . must necessarily be carried on collectively, and that because of this necessity men must surrender and submit themselves wholly to society so far as the production of wealth is concerned. Indeed, the possession of the greatest possible amount of temporal goods is esteemed so highly, that man's higher goods, not excepting liberty, must, they claim, be subordinated and even sacrificed to the exigencies of the most efficient production. . . . Society, therefore, as the socialist conceives it, is, on the one hand, impossible and unthinkable without the use of compulsion of the most excessive kind; on the other, it fosters a false liberty, since in such a scheme no place is found for true social authority, which is not based on temporal and material advantages, but descends from God alone, the Creator and last end of all things." *Quadragesimo anno,* p. 221, #118 and 119.

PIUS XI: "Free competition has killed itself. Economic domination has taken the place of untrammeled trade. Unbridled ambition for domination has succeeded the desire for gain; the whole economic life has become hard, cruel, and relentless in a ghastly way. . . . The State, which should be the supreme arbiter, ruling in kingly fashion far above all party contention, intent only upon justice and the common good, has become instead a slave, bound over to the service of human passion and greed." *Quadragesimo anno,* p. 217, #109.

PIUS XII: "Taught by bitter experience, they are more aggressive in opposing the concentration of dictatorial power that cannot be censured or touched, and call for a system of government more in keeping with the dignity and liberty of the citizens." *Christmas Message,* 1944.

PIUS XII: "Totalitarianism . . . grants to the civil power an unwarranted scope, determining and fixing, both in regard to form and content, every sphere of activity and so confining every legitimate individual life, whether personal, local, or professional, within a mechanical unity or collectivity conceived in terms of nation, race, or class.

"Equally unsatisfactory in regard to the same vital requirements is that conception of the civil power which may be styled 'authoritarian,' for this shuts out citizens from any effective share or influence in the formation of the social will. It consequently splits the nation into two categories, that of rulers and that of ruled, whose relations to each other are reduced to a purely mechanical kind, governed by force, or else based upon purely biological considerations." *Allocution to the Auditors and Other Officials of the Sacred Roman Rota,* October 2, 1945.

Q. *Are there any guarantees against the arbitrary exercise of power on the part of the State?*

A. The imitation by human laws of those which are eternal, the respect of a clear juridical order, protected by an independent juridical power, the duty on the part of the State to repair the damage done to private citizens by its action, the control by those ruled over those ruling them, constitute effective guarantees against the arbitrary exercise of power on the part of the State.

LEO XIII: "The liberty of those who are in authority does not consist in the power to lay unreasonable and capricious commands upon their subjects . . . but instead the binding force of human laws lies in the fact that they are to be regarded as applications of the eternal law, and are incapable of sanctioning anything which is not contained in the eternal law, as in the principle of all law." *Libertas,* p. 121, #7.

PIUS XII: "That social life, such as God willed it, may attain its scope, it needs a juridical order to support it from without, to defend and protect it. The function of this juridical order is not to dominate but to serve, to help the development and increase of society's vitality in the rich multiplicity of its ends, leading all the individual energies to their perfection in peaceful competition, and defending them with appropriate and honest means against all that may militate against those who only by this means can be held within the noble discipline of social life." *Christmas Message,* 1942.

PIUS XII: "The juridical order has, besides, the high and difficult scope of insuring harmonious relations both between individuals and between societies, and within these. This scope will be reached if legislators will abstain from following those perilous theories and practices, so harmful to communities and to their spirit of union, which derive their origin and promulgation from false postulates. Among such postulates we must count the juridical positivism which attributes a deceptive majesty to the setting up of purely human laws, and which leaves the way open for a fatal divorce of law from morality. . . . There is, besides, the conception which claims for particular nations or classes, the juridical instinct as the final imperative and the norm from which there is no appeal; finally, there are those various theories which, differing among themselves, and deriving from opposite ideologies, agree in considering the State, or a group which represents it, as an absolute and supreme entity, exempt from central control and from criticism even when its theoretical and practical postulates result in, and offend by, their open denial of essential tenets of the human Christian conscience." *Christmas Message*, 1942.

PIUS XII: "The relations of man to man, of the individual to society, to authority, to civil duties, the relations of society and of authority to the individual, should be placed on a firm juridic footing and be guarded, when the need arises, by the authority of the courts. This supposes: 1) a tribunal and a judge who take their directions from a clearly formulated and defined right; 2) clear juridical norms which may not be overturned by unwarranted appeals to a supposed popular sentiment or by merely utilitarian considerations; 3) the recognition of the principle that even the State and the functionaries and organizations depending on it are obliged to repair and to withdraw measures which are harmful to the liberty, property, honor, progress and health of the individuals." *Christmas Message*, 1942.

PIUS XII: "Had there been the possibility of censuring and correcting the actions of public authority, the world would not have been dragged into the vortex of a disastrous war . . . and . . . to avoid for the future the repetition of such a catastrophe, we must vest efficient guarantees in the people itself." *Christmas Message,* 1944.

The Citizen in Public Life

68

Q. *Must the citizen take an active part in public life?*

A. The citizen, man or woman, has a special obligation to take an active part in public life, for in so doing he cooperates in the attainment of the common good.

PIUS XI: "No citizen can remain aloof from political life when it concerns the common good and not the interest of each private individual." *Address to Italian Catholic Men,* October 30, 1926.

PIUS XI: "Every good citizen is obliged to make the best possible use of politics, particularly the Catholic citizen, because the profession of the Catholic faith demands that he be an upright citizen." *Peculiari quadam.*

LEO XIII: "It is also of great moment to the public welfare to take a prudent part in the business of municipal administration. . . . Furthermore it is in general fitting and salutary that Catholics should extend their efforts beyond this restricted sphere, and give their attention to national politics. . . . To take no share in public matters would be equally as wrong . . . as not to have concern for, or not to bestow labor upon, the common good." *Immortale Dei,* p. 87, #22.

PIUS XII: "Every woman . . . has the duty, the strict

obligation of conscience not to remain aloof, to enter into action (in the form and manner suitable to each one's condition) to contain the doctrines which threaten the family, to oppose those doctrines which are bent on uprooting its very foundations, to prepare, organize and effect its restoration." *Address to Catholic Women,* October 21, 1945.

69

Q. *Does a Catholic citizen have a particular obligation to take active part in public life?*

A. In view of his preparation and for the defense of the religious interests in a special manner entrusted to him, a Catholic has a special obligation to take an active part in public life, particularly in elections.

Pius X: "The present constitution of states offers indiscriminately to all the right to influence public opinion, and Catholics, with due respect for the obligations imposed by the law of God and the precepts of the Church, can certainly use this to their advantage. In such a way they can prove themselves as capable as others (in fact more capable than others) by cooperating in the material and civil welfare of the people. In so doing they shall acquire that authority and prestige which will make them capable of defending and promoting the highest good; namely, that of the soul." *Il fermo proposito.*

Pius X: "This . . . [the supreme good of society] places a duty on all Catholics to prepare themselves prudently and seriously for political life. . . ." *Il fermo proposito.*

Pius X: "The . . . principles which regulate the conscience of every true Catholic must be inculcated and put into practice. Above all else he must remember to be and to act in every circumstance as a true Catholic,

accepting and fulfilling public offices with the firm and
constant resolution of promoting by every means the
social and economic welfare of the country and particularly of the people, according to the maxims of a
truly Christian civilization, and at the same time defending the supreme interests of the Church, which are those
of religion and justice." *Il fermo proposito.*

Pius XI: "The right formation of the perfect Christian
and citizen, in which the supernatural ennobles all the
talents and actions and exalts them, contains also, as is
natural, the fulfillment of civil and social duties . . .
[such as] not to pass over his right to vote when the
good of the Church or of the country requires it." *Nos
es muy conocida.*

70

Q. *With what purpose in view must Catholics take
an active part in public life?*

A. Catholics must take an active part in public life
in order to give it a Christian direction and to
help civil power serve the true common good.

Leo XIII: Catholics participating in public life "assume
not the responsibility of approving what is blameworthy
in the actual methods of government, but seek to turn
these very methods, so far as possible, to the genuine
and true public good, and to use their best endeavours
at the same time to infuse as it were into all the veins of
the State the healthy sap and blood of Christian wisdom and virtue." *Immortale Dei,* p. 87, #22.

71

Q. *How shall Catholics take an active part in public life?*

A. Catholics shall take an active part in public life

by an open profession of their faith, without false prudence or foolish temerity.

LEO XIII: "Those who are called to bear a part in public life are menaced by two dangers which are to be avoided with all vigilance: prudence, falsely so called, and rashness. For some there are who doubt of the expediency of facing and opposing wickedness when successful, for fear, as they allege, lest the evildoers should be still further irritated. Are such men on the side of the Church, or are they against it? It would be hard to say. They profess Catholic doctrine, at the same time that they would have the Church give free play to heretical opinions. They complain of the decline of faith and of the decay of morals; yet they do not care to practice a remedy; nay, they often intensify such evils, either by excessive lenity or by a mischievous deceit. They would allow no man to suggest a doubt as to their devotion to the Apostolic See, yet they are never without some grievance against the Sovereign Pontiff. Their prudence is such as the Apostle St. Paul calls 'the wisdom of the flesh' and the 'death' of the soul. . . . Thus all who love wisdom according to the flesh . . . not only are useless in resisting the onslaught of the hosts of evil, but make the way readier for their coming. . . . Others, on the contrary, in no small numbers, whether moved by a false zeal, or still more blameably, by the affectation of feelings belied by their practice, assume to themselves a part to which they have no right. They would subject the government of the Church to their own ideas and to their own will, and with difficulty endure and unwillingly allow anything different from them. Such men as these spend their strength vainly and are not less blameworthy. To act thus is not to follow lawful authority, but to go in advance of it." *Sapientiae christianae*, p. 157, #18; p. 158, #19.

LEO XIII: "First and foremost it is the duty of all

Catholics worthy of the name and wishful to be known as most loving children of the Church, to reject without swerving whatever is inconsistent with so fair a title; to make use of popular institutions, so far as can honestly be done, for the advancement of truth and righteousness; to strive that liberty of action shall not transgress the bounds marked out by nature and the law of God; to endeavour to bring back all civil society to the pattern and form of Christianity which We have described. It is barely possible to lay down any fixed method by which such purposes are to be attained, because the means adopted must suit places and times widely differing from one another." *Immortale Dei*, p. 88, #23.

72

Q. *What evil would the abstention of Catholics from public life produce?*

A. By abstaining from public life, particularly from elections, Catholics would abandon the fate of the State in the hands of men whose opinions could not assure the State of activities having a sound Christian inspiration.

LEO XIII: "Furthermore it is in general fitting and salutary that Catholics should extend their efforts beyond this restricted sphere, and give their attention to national politics . . . while if they hold aloof, men whose principles offer but small guarantee for the welfare of the State will the more readily seize the reins of government. This would tend also to the injury of the Christian religion, forasmuch as those would come into power who are badly disposed towards the Church, and those who are willing to befriend her would be deprived of all influence. It follows therefore clearly that Catholics have just reasons for taking part in the conduct of public affairs." *Immortale Dei*, p. 87, #22.

Pius X: "In fact, those who aim at destroying religion and society, seek before any other thing to assume control of the government and make their own laws." *Inter catholicos.*

73

Q. *In the present conditions, by what directives must the public activities of a citizen be inspired?*

A. In order that civil society may be redirected to the promotion of the common good, the citizen must concur in returning full respect to the human person, in rejecting any form of materialism, in returning to labor the place assigned to it by God, in reintegrating the juridical order, in returning the State to the service of society and the individual.

Pius XII: "He who would have the Star of Peace shine out and stand over society, 1) should cooperate, for his part, in giving back to the human person the dignity given to it by God from the very beginning; he should favour social institutions in which a full personal responsibility is assured and guaranteed. . . . He should uphold respect for and the practical realization of . . . the fundamental personal rights. 2) He should reject every form of materialism. . . . He should strive to understand society as an intrinsic unity, which has grown up and matured under the guidance of Providence. . . . He should defend the indissolubility of matrimony; he should give to the family. . . light and air. . . . 3) He should give to work the place assigned to it by God from the beginning . . . a just wage . . . an assured, even if modest, private property for all classes of society . . . higher education for the children of the working class who are specially endowed with intelligence and good will. . . promote the care and the practice of the social spirit in one's immediate neighborhood, in the district, the province, the people and the nations. . . . 4) He should collaborate towards a complete rehabilitation of the juridical order. . . . 5) He should cooperate towards the setting up of a State conception and practice founded on reasonable discipline, exalted kindliness and a responsible Christian spirit. . . . He should help to restore the State and its power to the service of human society, to the full recognition of the respect due to the human person and his efforts to attain his eternal destiny. He should apply and devote himself to dispelling the errors which aim at causing the State and its authority to deviate from the path of morality, at severing them from the eminently ethical bond which links them to individual and social life. . . . He should work for the recognition and diffusion of the truth which teaches, even in matters of this world, that the deepest meaning, the ultimate moral basis and the universal validity of 'reigning' lies in 'serving.'" *Christmas Message,* 1942.

74

Q. *Is the existence of many parties lawful?*

A. The diversity of political opinions and the resulting existence of political parties, with due protection for truth and justice, is lawful, provided they do not degenerate into factions detrimental to the common good.

LEO XIII: "We cannot doubt that in the political world there is an honourable strife, when under the principles of truth and justice men endeavour to make those opinions prevail which conduce most to the common good." *Sapientiae christianae,* p. 155, #15.

PIUS XI: "Further, there is the strife of political parties, with their divergent views, not in reality seeking the common good, but rather their own advantages at the expense of others. Hence come plots, attacks even on public ministers, threats, open revolts, and other excesses of a similar kind." *Ubi arcano*, p. 8, #9.

75

Q. *What is the position of the Church with reference to political parties?*

A. The Church recognizes the right for everyone to have his own opinions in purely political matters, with due safeguard for truth and justice; however, she claims it as her right and duty to remain free from all parties.

Leo XIII: "First of all, 1) every citizen is free to maintain his own opinion in merely political matters, provided that in so doing he does not act contrary to the principles of religion and justice; 2) every citizen is free to uphold his own point of view by legitimate and honest means; 3) those citizens are in error who fail to make a proper distinction between sacred matters and those which are purely civil; 4) whoever uses religion for the interests of his own political party is in error." *Pergrata nobis.*

Leo XIII: "And since her [the Church's] society is not only perfect, but is also placed above every human society, she, in the fulfillment of her right and her office, firmly refuses to side with any parties, and to bend the knee to the fleeting and changeable politics of the civil order. . . . But to sully the Church by party strife or to desire to make her an ally in overcoming opponents in such strife, would be the work of men who rashly abuse religion. On the contrary, religion should be held sacred and immaculate by all. In the very enforcement of state discipline, a matter impossible to be separated from the laws and duties of religion, the interests of

Christianity should particularly be borne in mind; and wherever these should seem to be in danger from the attacks of opponents, all strife must be stopped, and the defense of religion undertaken in full agreement together, since religion is the highest good of the community by which every act should be regulated. We think it necessary to expound this somewhat more fully." *Sapientiae christianae*, p. 155, #15.

76

Q. *May Catholics belong to any political party?*

A. Catholics may belong to any political party whose program does not contain principles contrary to religion and justice and whose activities give assurance of protection for the rights of God and the human person, the family and the Church. However, they must be ready to settle all partisan controversies whenever the interests of religion and the common good are at stake.

PIUS XI: "Individually, Catholics are permitted to belong to political organizations, when the program activities of such organizations offer the necessary assurance that the rights of God and those of human conscience will be protected." *Letter to the Patriarch of Lisbon.*

LEO XIII: "Men of opposite parties, though differing in all else, should be agreed unanimously in this: that religion in the State should be preserved in all its integrity. To this noble and indispensable aim, all who love the Catholic religion ought, as if bound by a compact, to direct all their efforts; they should be somewhat silent about their various political opinions, which they are, however, at perfect liberty to ventilate in their proper place." *Cum multa.*

Pius X: "In the exercise of their right of election, Catholics can engage by legitimate means in the triumph of their point of view, which appears to them to be the best; but it is also necessary that they check any partisan spirit lest the interests of religion and the fundamental rights of the common good be overlooked. A division among Catholics in times of election is a grave danger. Such division has often brought cruel abuses and persecutions upon the Church. . . . In any case, when electoral disputes involve religious interests or the more important interests of the country, there arises the duty to vote for the candidate who is more apt to give aid to Catholics and other men of good will toward proper action, but at the same time all personal or party ambitions in such cases must be set aside." *Inter catholicos.*

77

Q. *Do elected officials and public administrators have any special duties?*

A. Elected officials and public administrators have the duty to exercise their functions for the good of the country and the people, according to the principles of religion and justice.

Pius X: "Accepting and fulfilling public offices (every true Catholic must do so) with the firm and constant resolution of promoting by every means the social and economic welfare of the country and particularly of the people, according to the maxims of a truly Christian civilization, and at the same time defending the supreme interests of the Church, which are those of religion and justice. . . ." *Il fermo proposito.*

Pius XII: "To secure effective action, to win esteem and trust, every legislative body should—as experience shows beyond doubt—gather within a group of select men, spiritually eminent and of strong character, who shall look upon themselves as the representatives of the entire people and not the mandatories of a mob, whose interests are often unfortunately made to prevail over the true needs of the common good—a select group of men not restricted to any profession or social standing but reflecting every phase of the people's life; men chosen for their solid Christian convictions, straight and steady judgment, with a sense of the practical and equitable, true to themselves in all circumstances; men of clear and sound principles, with sound and clear-cut proposals to make; men above all capable, in virtue of the authority that emanates from their untarnished consciences and radiates widely from them, to be leaders and heads especially in times when the pressing needs of the moment excite the people's impressionability unduly, and render it more liable to be led astray and get lost; men who feel themselves doubly under the obligation to send circulating through the beings of the people and of the State, burning with a thousand fevers, the spiritual antidote of clear views, kindly interest, a justice equally sympathetic to all, and a bias toward national unity and concord in a sincere spirit of brotherhood." *Christmas Message,* 1944.

Pius XI: "State functionaries and all employees are obliged in conscience to perform their duties faithfully and unselfishly, imitating the brilliant example of distinguished men of the past and of our own day, who with unremitting labor sacrificed their all for the good of their country." *Divini Redemptoris,* p. 372, #82.

Part Four

The Church and Its Relations
with
The State

―――――――

Chapter   VII.   *Nature, Ends and Power of the Church*
Chapter VIII.   *Relations Between Church and State*

Nature, Ends and Power of the Church

78

Q. *What is the Church?*

A. "The Church is a society of true Christians, that is, of baptized people who profess the faith and the doctrine of Jesus Christ, partake of His sacraments and obey the pastors established by Him" (from the Catechism of St. Pius X). The Church is a supernatural society as to its end and its means, and a perfect one in view of its capacity for autonomous and complete power of operation.

LEO XIII: "We must go yet more deeply into the nature of the Church, as being not a mere chance union of Christians, but as a society divinely constituted and wonderfully organized, having as its direct object to bestow peace and holiness on the soul; and since for this end it alone by divine gift possesses the necessary means, it has fixed laws, fixed functions, and in the direction of Christian peoples follows a method most consonant with its nature." *Sapientiae christianae*, p. 154, #13.

LEO XIII: "And yet [it] is supernatural and spiritual, on account of the end for which it was founded, and because of the means by which it aims to attaining that end. Hence it is distinguished from civil society and differs from it. And what is of the highest moment, it is a society chartered as of right divine, perfect in its nature and in its title, possessing in itself and by itself, through the will and loving kindness of its Founder, all needful provision for its maintenance and action." *Immortale Dei*, p. 70, #5.

Pius XII: "The Church is not a political, but a religious society." *Christmas Message*, 1951.

79

Q. *What is the end of the Church?*

A. The end of the Church is the eternal salvation of souls.

Leo XIII: "Consequently, as Jesus Christ came into the world that men 'might have life and have it more abundantly' (John 10:10), so also the Church has for her aim and end the eternal salvation of souls. Wherefore she is so endowed as to open wide her arms to all mankind, unhampered by any limit of either time or place." *Immortale Dei*, p. 69, #5.

80

Q. *Is the Church supreme in its own sphere of operation?*

A. In view of its end and its perfection the Church is subordinate to no other human society. It is supreme in its own field.

Leo XIII: "And just as the end at which the Church aims is by far the noblest of ends, so its authority is the most exalted of all authority, nor can it be looked upon as inferior to the civil power, or in any manner dependent upon it. To wish the Church to be subject to the civil power in the exercise of her duty is a great folly and a sheer injustice. Whenever this is the case, order is disturbed, for things natural are put above things supernatural." *Immortale Dei.* (Quoted in *The Church Speaks to the Modern World;* New York: Doubleday, Image Books.)

81

Q. *Does the Church have care only of the supernatural happiness of man?*

A. In order better to promote the eternal welfare of man, the Church concerns itself also with those aspects of human life having a relation with his eternal welfare.

PIUS XII: "It is . . . the indisputable competence of the Church, on that side of the social order where it meets and enters into contact with the moral order, to decide whether the bases of a given social system are in accord with the unchangeable order which God our Creator and Redeemer has shown us through the natural law and revelation." *Message on Pentecost,* 1941.

PIUS XI: "The Church does not separate a proper regard for temporal welfare from solicitude for the eternal. If she subordinates the former to the latter . . . she is nevertheless so far from being unconcerned with human affairs, so far from hindering civil progress and material advancement, that she actually fosters and promotes them in the most sensible and efficacious manner." *Divini Redemptoris,* p. 355, #33.

LEO XIII: "Hence the Pontiff must have the power authoritatively to judge of the meaning of Holy Scripture; what doctrines are in harmony with it and what at variance; and also to declare what is virtuous and what sinful, what is to be done and what avoided in the work of salvation." *Sapientiae christianae,* p. 153, #12.

Q. *What are the rights of the Church?*

A. The Church has the right to defend against any
   intruder its exclusive competence in matters
   regarding the sacraments and its doctrine. The
   exercise of this mission gives it exclusive competence in matters concerning matrimony and
   a supereminent competence in the field of
   education, besides the right to accept, possess
   and use as its own, goods which are necessary
   to its mission.

PIUS X: "It is the duty of the Church to provide for
man's spiritual life and to administer the sacraments, and
insofar as this is concerned no one for any reason whatsoever has the right to enter into this sacred field. For
this reason the Church has the right to oppose anyone
who by any arbitrary notion or unjust usurpation attempts to invade its domain. The Church has also the
right to teach the evangelical precepts. Being a society
of men, not of angels, the Church has the right to own
property and those goods given to it by the faithful for
its own material needs. It has the right to enjoy its
legitimate possessions for the fulfillment of its mission,
for the needs of the external cult, the construction of
churches, for its works of charity, and to be able to
continue and perpetuate its mission till the end of time."
Address to Pilgrims from Milan.

LEO XIII: "The Church, always and everywhere, has so
used her power with reference to the marriages of
Christians, that men have seen clearly how it belongs to
her as of native right; not being made hers by any human
grant, but given divinely to her by the will of her
Founder. . . . Since marriage, then, is holy by its power,
in its own nature, and of itself, it ought not to be

regulated and administered by the will of civil rulers, but by the divine authority of the Church, which alone in sacred matters professes the office of teaching." *Arcanum,* p. 31, #9, p. 33, #11.

Pius XI: The education of youth "belongs pre-eminently to the Church, by reason of a double title in the supernatural order, conferred exclusively upon her by God Himself: absolutely superior therefore to any other title in the natural order. The first title is founded upon the express mission and supreme authority to teach, given her by her divine Founder. . . . The second title is the supernatural motherhood. . . ." *Divini illius magistri.*

83

Q. *Why does the Church concern itself with social and economic questions?*

A. The Church legitimately concerns itself with economic and social questions because of their relation with moral and religious questions, and to facilitate the attainment of man's ultimate end.

Leo XIII: "The social question presents itself under more than one aspect: in fact, it involves elements of external and material well-being, but it is intimately bound with religion and morals." *Permoti Nos.*

Leo XIII: "For it is the opinion of some, which is caught up by the masses, that the social question, as they call it, is merely economic. The precise opposite is the truth. It is first of all moral and religious, and for that reason its solution is to be expected mainly from the moral law and the pronouncements of religion." *Graves de communi,* p. 234, #10.

Pius XI: "It is Our right and Our duty to deal authoritatively with social and economic problems. It is not, of course, the function of the Church to lead men to transient and perishable happiness only, but to that which is eternal. Indeed the Church believes that it would be wrong for her to interfere without just cause in such earthly concerns; but she never can relinquish her God-given task of interposing her authority, not indeed in technical matters, for which she has neither the equipment nor the mission, but all those that have a bearing on moral conduct. For the deposit of truth entrusted to Us by God, and Our weighty office of declaring, interpreting, and urging in season and out of season the entire moral law, demand that both social and economic questions be brought within Our supreme jurisdiction, insofar as they refer to moral issues.

"For, though economic order and moral discipline are guided each by its own principles in its own sphere, it is false that the two orders are so distinct and alien that the former in no way depends on the latter. The so-called laws of economics, derived from the nature of earthly goods and from the qualities of the human body and soul, determine what aims are unattainable or attainable in economic matters and what means are therefore necessary. On the other hand, reason itself clearly deduces from the nature of things and from the individual and social character of man, what is the end and object of the whole economic order assigned by God the Creator.

"For it is the moral law alone which commands us to seek in all our conduct our supreme and final end, and to strive in our specific actions for those ends which nature, or rather, the Author of Nature, has established for them, duly subordinating particular aims to our last end. If this law be faithfully obeyed, the result will be that particular economic aims, whether of society as a body or of individuals, will find their proper place within the universal order of ends, and as a consequence we shall be led by progressive stages to the final end of all,

God Himself, our highest and lasting good." *Quadragesimo anno*, pp. 191–192, #41–43.

Pius XII: "You know well that the social order is in many respects bound up with religious and moral questions, and dependent on them. In times of economic upheavals and social agitation, the Church has the right and the duty to give renewed expression to the Catholic teaching. This teaching is sufficiently broad to allow of its being adapted to the changing circumstances of the times without detriment to its immutable and enduring principles. No one can abandon it without danger to faith and morals. Hence, it is not permissible for any Catholic . . . to support social theories and questions which the Church has repudiated, or pronounced dangerous." *Address to Catholic Action Leaders*, April 29, 1945. (Quoted in *The London Tablet*.)

84

Q. *Why does the Church concern itself with political questions?*

A. Indifferent from a technical standpoint to political systems, diverse by reasons of time and territory, the Church is deeply interested in seeing to it that in all circumstances the changing of laws and constitutions does no harm to faith and morals, for this would hinder the individual in the pursuit of his own natural and supernatural ends, and the Church in fulfilling its own mission.

Pius XII: "In such strife of opinions the Church cannot be invoked to listen to one side more than to another. Within the divine laws given not only to the individual, but also to nations, there is a wide sphere in which the most varied forms of political life have ample freedom of expression. The effects of one or other political system, however, depend on circumstances and reasons which, considered in themselves, are beyond the scope of the Church's activity. As protector and prophet of faith and morality, the Church has only one interest and one desire, namely, to fulfill her educational mission and to carry religious teaching to all peoples without exception so that every nation may be enabled to avail itself of the principles laid down by Christianity in order to establish a dignified and spiritually ennobled life which is the source of real happiness." *Christmas Message*, 1940.

Leo XIII: "The Church has no care what form of government exists in a state, or by what customs the civil order of Christian nations is directed. Of the various kinds of government there is none of which she disapproves, so long as religion and moral discipline live untouched. For this reason the Church cannot but concern herself about the laws formulated in States, not for their connection with the government, but because they sometimes encroach on the right of the Church by passing their due bounds. Nay, it is a duty assigned by God to the Church to make resistance, if at any time the State does harm to religion, and to strive that the virtue of the Gospel shall influence the laws and institutions of peoples." *Sapientiae christianae*, pp. 155–156, #15, 16.

Pius XI: "The Church, indeed, does not assert a right of intervening without reason in the direction of temporal or purely political affairs. But, of her full right she claims that the civil power must not allege this as an excuse for placing obstacles in the way of those higher goods on which the salvation of man depends, for inflicting loss and injury through unjust laws and decrees, for impairing the divine constitution of the Church itself, or for trampling underfoot the sacred rights of God in civil society." *Ubi arcano*, p. 26, #61.

Q. *Can the Church flourish under any form of government?*

A. The Church can flourish under any form of government which would respect and protect the rights of justice and religion.

LEO XIII: "The precepts of the natural law and the Gospel, for the very reason that they transcend the vicissitudes of human existence, must necessarily be independent of any particular form of civil government and adapt themselves to all forms so long as these are not opposed to what is right and just. In themselves, they therefore are and remain completely outside of party rivalries and political changes, so that, under any kind of government, people may and ought to abide by those precepts, which bid them love God above all and their neighbors as themselves. This has ever been the morality of the Church. By it the Roman Pontiffs have constantly dealt with states, whatever might be their form of government." *Graves de communi*, p. 232, #6.

CHAPTER VIII

Relations Between Church and State

86

Q. *Are the Church and the State supreme in their own respective orders?*

A. The Church rules over things divine, while the State rules over things material, and both are supreme in their own respective orders.

LEO XIII: "The Almighty, therefore, has appointed the charge of the human race between two powers, the ecclesiastical and the civil, the one being set over divine, and the other over human, things. Each in its kind is supreme, each has fixed limits within which it is contained, limits which are defined by the nature and special object of the province of each. . . . But inasmuch as each of these two powers has authority over the same subjects, and inasmuch as one and the same thing under different aspects, but still remaining identically the same, might chance to fall under the jurisdiction and determination of both powers, God, who foresees all things and is Author alike of these two powers, has marked out the course of each in right correlation to the other. . . . Were this not so, deplorable contentions and conflicts would often arise. . . . But to deem thus of the wisdom and goodness of God would be most repugnant. . . . There must, accordingly, exist, between these two powers, a certain orderly connection." *Immortale Dei*, pp. 71–72, #6.

Leo XIII: "The nature and scope of that connection can be determined only, as We have laid down, by having regard to the nature of each power, and by taking account of the relative excellence and nobleness of their purpose. One of the two has for its proximate and chief object the well-being of this mortal life; the other the everlasting joys of heaven. Whatever, therefore, in things human is of a sacred character, whatever belongs either of its own nature or by reason of the end to which it is referred, to the salvation of souls, or to the worship of God, is subject to the power and judgment of the Church. Whatever is to be ranged under the civil and political order is rightly subject to the civil authority. . . . There are, nevertheless, occasions when another method of concord is available, for the sake of peace and liberty. We mean when rulers of States and the Roman Pontiff come to an understanding touching some special matter." *Immortale Dei*, pp. 72–73, #6.

87

Q. *Is collaboration between Church and State natural and necessary?*

A. For the good of humanity, collaboration between Church and State in keeping with the plans of Providence in regard to society is necessary.

Leo XIII: "Yet no one doubts that Jesus Christ, the Founder of the Church, willed her sacred power to be distinct from the civil power, and each power to be free and unshackled in its own sphere: with this condition, however—a condition good alike for both, and of advantage to all men—that union and concord should be maintained between them; and that in such questions as are, though in different ways, of common right and authority, the power to which secular matters have been entrusted should happily and becomingly depend on the other power which has in its charge the interests of heaven. In such arrangement and harmony is found not only the best line of action for each power, but also the most opportune and efficacious method of helping men in all that pertains to their life here, and to their hope of salvation hereafter." *Arcanum,* p. 42, #22.

LEO XIII: "And, what is still more important . . . is the fact that, although the civil authority has not the same proximate end as the spiritual, nor proceeds on the same lines, nevertheless in the exercise of their separate powers these authorities must occasionally meet. For their subjects are the same: and not infrequently they deal with the same objects, though in different ways. Whenever this occurs, since a state of conflict is absurd and manifestly repugnant to the most wise ordinance of God, there must necessarily exist some order or mode of procedure to remove the occasions of difference and contention, and to secure harmony in all things." *Libertas,* p. 127, #14.

PIUS XI: "For the preservation of the moral order neither the laws nor the sanctions of the temporal power are sufficient, nor is the beauty of virtue and the expounding of its necessity. Religious authority must enter in to enlighten the mind, to direct the will, and to strengthen human frailty by the assistance of divine grace. Such an authority is found nowhere save in the Church instituted by Christ the Lord. Hence We earnestly exhort in the Lord all those who hold the reins of power that they firmly establish and maintain harmony and friendship with this Church of Christ so that, through the united activity and energy of both powers, the tremendous evils, fruits of those wanton liberties which assail both marriage and the family and are a menace to both Church and State, may be effectively frustrated." *Casti connubii,* p. 171, #130.

PIUS XI: "One supreme authority can be united and

associated with the other without detriment to the rights and supreme power of either, thus protecting Christian parents from pernicious evils and menacing ruin." *Casti connubii,* p. 172, #133.

88

Q. *Does the State have any duties toward the Church?*

A. As mentioned above (cf. Q. 59), the State has the obligation not to hinder the Church in the fulfillment of its mission, and to respect its teachings in civil laws.

Pius XI: "At the same time the State must allow the Church full liberty to fulfill her divine and spiritual mission, and this in itself will be an effectual contribution to the rescue of nations from the dread torment of the present hour." *Divini Redemptoris,* p. 372, #83.

Leo XIII: "To exclude the Church, founded by God Himself from the business of life, from the power of making laws, from the training of youth, from domestic society, is a grave and fatal error." *Immortale Dei,* p. 81, #15.

89

Q. *Can the Church remain indifferent to the laws of the State?*

A. When the laws of the State infringe upon the Church's natural and positive divine rights, the Church cannot remain indifferent, for by such infringements the State goes beyond the competence allowed to civil power.

Leo XIII: "For this reason the Church cannot but concern herself about the laws formulated in States, not for their connexion with the government, but because they sometimes encroach on the right of the Church by passing their due bonds." *Sapientiae christianae*, p. 156, #16.

90

Q. *In order to prevent conflicts, can the respective jurisdictions of the Church and the State be determined?*

A. In view of each one's respective ends, all that concerns the salvation of souls and divine worship falls under the jurisdiction of the Church, whereas all that regards the material common good, as a civil and positive element, falls under the jurisdiction of the State.

Leo XIII: "One of the two has for its proximate and chief object the well-being of this mortal life; the other the everlasting joys of heaven. Whatever, therefore, in things human is of a sacred character, whatever belongs either of its own nature or by reason of the end to which it is referred, to the salvation of souls, or to the worship of God, is subject to the power and judgment of the Church. Whatever is to be ranged under the civil and political order is rightly subject to the civil authority. Jesus Christ has Himself given command that what is Caesar's is to be rendered to Caesar, and that what belongs to God is to be rendered to God." *Immortale Dei*, p. 72, #6.

91

Q. *Are there any fields of jurisdiction common to the Church and the State?*

A. Since the Church and the State both exercise power over man, under different aspects man can be the object of discipline on the part of both powers. In such cases there arise fields of mixed jurisdiction.

Leo XIII: "But inasmuch as each of these two powers has authority over the same subjects, and inasmuch as one and the same thing under different aspects, but still remaining identically the same, might chance to fall under the jurisdiction and determination of both powers, God, who foresees all things and is Author alike of these two powers, has marked out the course of each in right correlation to the other." *Immortale Dei,* p. 71, #6.

92

Q. *What are the most important cases of mixed jurisdiction?*

A. The principal cases of mixed jurisdiction regard matrimony and the education of youth.

Leo XIII: The Church "is not unaware, and never calls in doubt, that the sacrament of Marriage, since it was instituted for the preservation and increase of the human race, has a necessary relation to various circumstances of life, which, though connected with marriage, belong to the civil order, and about which the State rightly makes strict enquiry and justly promulgates decrees." *Arcanum,* p. 42, #21.

Pius XI: "The Church of Jesus Christ has never contested the rights and the duties of the State concerning the education of its citizens and We Ourselves have recalled and proclaimed them in Our recent Encyclical Letter on the Christian Education of Youth; rights and duties which are unchallengeable as long as they remain within the limits of the State's proper competency, a competency which in its turn is clearly indicated and determined by the missions of the State, missions certainly not only bodily and material, but missions that by the very necessity of their character are contained within the limits of the natural, the earthly and the temporary." *Non abbiamo bisogno.*

PIUS XI: "What we object to, and what we must object to, is the intentional and systematically fomented opposition which is set up between these educational purposes and those of religion. . . . He who sings the song of loyalty to his earthly country must not, in disloyalty to God, to his Church, to his eternal country, become a deserter and a traitor." *Mit brennender Sorge.*

PIUS XI: "The education of youth is precisely one of those matters that belong both to the Church and to the State, though in different ways; therefore . . . between the two powers there must reign a well-ordered harmony." *Divini illius magistri.*

93

Q. *Is harmony between the two powers possible even in matters of mixed jurisdiction?*

A. Harmony between the two powers even in matters of mixed jurisdiction is both natural and necessary.

LEO XIII: "In matters, however, of mixed jurisdiction, it is in the highest degree consonant to nature, as also to the designs of God, that far from one of the powers separating itself from the other, or still less coming into conflict with it, complete harmony, such as is suited to the end for which each power exists, should be preserved between them." *Immortale Dei,* p. 83, #17.

94

Q. *In our times, how is collaboration between Church and State regulated?*

A. In our days, collaboration between Church and State is regulated by appropriate pacts, called concordats.

Leo XIII: "There are, nevertheless, occasions when another method of concord is available, for the sake of peace and liberty. We mean when rulers of States and the Roman Pontiff come to an understanding touching some special matter. At such times the Church gives signal proof of her motherly love by showing the greatest possible kindliness and indulgence." *Immortale Dei*, pp. 72–73, #6.

95

Q. *What are the current errors with regard to relations between Church and State?*

A. Ignoring the nature of man, of the Church and of the State, many insist on absolute separation between Church and State. Others subject the Church to the jurisdiction of the State; others still demand of the Church a tolerance that is not according to justice.

Leo XIII: "Many wish the State to be separated from the Church wholly and entirely, so that in regard to every right of human society, in institutions, customs, and laws the offices of State, and the education of youth, they would pay no more regard to the Church than if she did not exist; and, at most, would allow the citizens individually to attend to their religion in private if so minded. Against such as these, all the arguments by which We disprove the principle of separation of Church and State are conclusive; with this superadded, that it is absurd that the citizens should respect the Church, while the State may hold her in contempt.

"Others oppose not the existence of the Church, nor

indeed could they; yet they despoil her of the nature and rights of a perfect society; and maintain that it does not belong to her to legislate, to judge, or to punish, but only to exhort, to advise, and to rule her subjects in accordance with their own consent and will. By such opinion they pervert the nature of this divine Society, and attenuate and narrow its authority, its office of teacher, and its whole efficiency; and at the same time they aggrandize the power of the civil government to such extent as to subject the Church of God to the empire and sway of the State, like any voluntary association of citizens. To refute completely such teaching, the arguments often used by the defenders of Christianity, and set forth by Us, especially in the Encyclical Letter *Immortale Dei*, are of great avail; for by those arguments it is proved that, by a divine provision, all the rights which essentially belong to a society that is legitimate, supreme, and perfect in all its parts, exist in the Church.

"Lastly, there remain those who, while they do not approve the separation of Church and State, think nevertheless that the Church ought to adapt herself to the times, and conform to what is required by the modern system of government. Such an opinion is sound, if it is to be understood of some equitable adjustment consistent with truth and justice; insofar, namely, that the Church, in the hope of some great good, may show herself indulgent, and may conform to the times within the limits which her sacred office permits. But it is not so in regard to practices and doctrines which a perversion of morals and a warped judgment have unlawfully introduced. Religion, truth, and justice, must ever be maintained; and, as God has entrusted these great and sacred matters to the care of the Church, she can never be so unfaithful to her office as to dissemble in regard to what is false or unjust, or to connive at what is hurtful to religion." *Libertas*, p. 137, #27–29.

Q. *What are the effects of an erroneous doctrine regarding relations between Church and State?*

A. Absolute separation and persecution are the ultimate effects of an erroneous doctrine regarding relations between Church and State.

Leo XIII: "For when the management of public business is in harmony with doctrines of such a kind, the Catholic religion is allowed a standing in civil society equal only, or inferior, to societies alien from it; no regard is paid to the laws of the Church. [She] finds herself forbidden to take any part in the instruction of the people. With reference to matters that are of twofold jurisdiction, they who administer the civil power lay down the law at their own will, and in matters that appertain to religion, defiantly put aside the most sacred decrees of the Church. They claim jurisdiction over the marriages of Catholics, even over the bond as well as the unity and the indissolubility of matrimony. They lay hands on the goods of the clergy, contending that the Church cannot possess property. Lastly, they treat the Church with such arrogance that, rejecting entirely her title to the nature and rights of a perfect society, they hold that she differs in no respect from other societies in the State, and for this reason possesses no right nor any legal power of action, save that which she holds by the concession and favour of the government. If in any State the Church retains her own right—and this with the approval of the civil law, owing to an agreement publicly entered into by the two powers—men forthwith begin to cry out that matters affecting the Church must be separated from those of the State. . . . And as the Church, unable to abandon her chief and most sacred duties, cannot patiently put up with this, and asks that the pledge given to her be fully and scrupulously acted up to, contentions frequently arise between the ecclesiastical and the civil power, of which the issue commonly is, that the weaker power is beaten by the one which is stronger in human resources." *Immortale Dei*, pp. 77 and 78, #11.

Translator's Note:

In the treatment of this very important subject, Mr. Fanfani follows the Church's traditional doctrine that full cooperation is natural and necessary in the relations between Church and State.

In support of this doctrine, Mr. Fanfani quotes extensively from important papal documents of two very eminent pontiffs, Pope Leo XIII (*Arcanum, Libertas, Immortale Dei, Sapientiae christianae*) and Pope Pius XI (*Casti connubii, Divini Redemptoris, Non abbiamo bisogno, Mit Brennender Sorge*).

However, since this problem is of greatest interest to United States Catholics, we should like to point out that in recent years the question of Church-State relations has been the object of considerable study on both sides of the Atlantic. It is the aim of this study to establish the basis for a Catholic doctrine on religious tolerance in higher motives and loftier principles than in the traditional "error has no rights" thesis held in some Catholic circles. Nor are eminent advocates of this new treatment wanting by any means; among others, there are François Charriere, Bishop of Lausanne, Switzerland, Yves de la Briére, in Europe, Father John Courtney Murray, S.J., in the United States.

The latest contribution to this study comes from a very outstanding churchman, Giacomo Cardinal Lercaro, Archbishop of Bologna, in his remarkable essay, "Religious Tolerance in Catholic Tradition," which appears in the January–February (1960) issue of the *Catholic Mind*. It deserves the greatest attention.

The Cardinal's essay and its bibliographical references indicate at least that "a clarification of ideas on civil liberties is well under way in Europe." But more than that, they lend support and encouragement to the study of a problem the solution of which is of interest to a vast number of people in the United States as well as abroad.

Part Five

The Economic Order

Chapter   IX.   *Aspects and Causes of the Present Economic Disorder*

Chapter   X.   *Remedies Which Further Aggravate the Contemporary Economic Disorder*

Chapter   XI.   *The Church and the Reorganization of Economic Life*

Chapter XII.   *Natural Characteristics of the Economic Order*

Chapter XIII.   *Counsels of the Church for the Reforming of Institutions and Practices in the Economic Field*

Aspects and Causes of the Present Economic Disorder

97

Q. *Is the present economic order in keeping with the rights of the individual and the common good?*

A. Despite undeniable merits, the present-day economic order has very grave weaknesses which can be summed up in the concentration of riches in the hands of a few overpowerful manipulators of public affairs, and an aggravated state of poverty of the masses. Both are causes of unbalance, of national and international struggles, insecurity, moral distress, and great difficulties in the development of the human person.

PIUS XI: "But it is the capitalist economic regime which, with the world-wide diffusion of industry, has penetrated everywhere . . . intimately affecting them by its advantages, inconveniences, and vices. . . .

"In the first place . . . it is patent that in our days not alone is wealth accumulated, but immense power and despotic economic domination are concentrated in the hands of a few, and that those few are frequently not the owners, but only the trustees and directors of invested funds, which they administer at their good pleasure.

"This domination becomes particularly irresistible when exercised by those who, because they hold and control money, are able to govern credit and determine its allotment, for that reason supplying, so to speak, the lifeblood to the entire economic body, and grasping, as it were, in their hands the very soul of production, so that no one dare breathe against their will.

"This accumulation of resources and power, the characteristic note of the modern economic order, is a natural result of limitless free competition which permits the survival only of those who are the strongest, which often means those who fight most relentlessly, who pay least heed to the dictates of conscience.

"This concentration of power has in turn led to a threefold struggle. First, there is the struggle for dictatorship in the economic sphere itself; then, the fierce battle to acquire control of the state, so that its resources and authority may be abused in the economic struggles; and finally, the clash between states themselves. . . .

". . . and you lament the ultimate consequences of this individualistic spirit in economic affairs. Free competition has killed itself. Economic domination has taken the place of untrammeled trade. Unbridled ambition for domination has succeeded the desire for gain; the whole economic life has become hard, cruel, and relentless in a ghastly way.

"Furthermore, the intermingling and scandalous confusing of the duties and offices of civil authority and of economics have produced crying evils and have gone so far as to degrade the majesty of the State. The State which should be the supreme arbiter, ruling in kingly fashion far above all party contention, intent only upon justice and the common good, has become instead a slave, bound over to the service of human passion and greed.

"As regards the relations of peoples among themselves,

a double stream has issued forth from this one fountainhead: on the one hand, economic nationalism or even economic imperialism; on the other, a not less noxious and detestable internationalism or international imperialism in financial affairs, which holds that where a man's fortune is, there is his country." *Quadragesimo anno*, pp. 215–217 *passim*.

LEO XIII: ". . . wage earners, . . . are, undoubtedly, among the weak and necessitous. . . ." *Rerum novarum*, p. 189, #29.

PIUS XII: "Today the production and consumption of economic goods take place in a society which does not know how to impart progress, measure, harmony or stability. Here is the source from which derives—and perhaps even more from this reason than from the outward circumstances of our time—that sense of uncertainty, that lack of security, which one observes in the present-day economy; uncertainty which not even hope in the future can render more tolerable." *Address to Italian Catholic Workers Association*, May 14, 1953.

98

Q. *What factors have produced the contemporary economic disorder?*

A. False philosophical and moral principles, a political development inadequate to the technological development, uncontrolled freedom for the rich, inadequate defense of the poor, and revolutionary doctrine have contributed to cause the unreasonableness and the injustices of the contemporary economic disorder.

LEO XIII: "These disputes arise in the first instance from widespread philosophical and moral error. The scientific resources of the age, increased facilities of communication, and appliances of all kinds for economizing labour and making it more productive have resulted in a keener struggle for existence. Through the harmful influence of agitators the gulf between rich and poor has been widened. . . ." *Graves de communi*, p. 229, #1.

LEO XIII: "For the effect of civil change and revolution has been to divide society into two widely different castes. On the one side there is the party which holds the power because it holds the wealth; which has in its own benefit and its own purposes all the sources of supply, and which is powerfully represented in the councils of the State itself. On the other side there is the needy and powerless multitude, sore and suffering, always ready for disturbance." *Rerum novarum*, p. 194, #35.

LEO XIII: "For the ancient workingmen's guilds were destroyed in the last century, and no other organization took their place. . . . It has come to pass that workingmen have been given over, isolated and defenseless, to the callousness of employers and the greed of unrestrained competition. The evil has been increased by rapacious usury, which, although more than once condemned by the Church, is nevertheless, under a different form but with the same guilt, still practiced by avaricious and grasping men. And to this must be added the custom of working by contract, and the concentration of so many branches of trade in the hands of a few individuals, so that a small number of very rich men have been able to lay upon the masses of the poor a yoke little better than slavery itself." *Rerum novarum*, p. 168, #2.

PIUS XII: "In the social field the counterfeiting of God's plan has gone to its very roots by deforming the divine image of man. . . . As an outgrowth of this, which came to wield increasing power over a long period of years . . . was that narrowly individualistic order which today is in serious crisis almost everywhere. But the more recent innovators have provided no better results. Starting from the same mistaken premises and taking the downward path in another direction, they have led to no less disastrous consequences, including the complete overthrow of the Divine Order, contempt for the dignity of the human person, the denial of the most sacred and fundamental freedoms, the domination of a single class over the others, the enslavement of all persons and property in a totalitarian state and the legalization of violence, and militant atheism." *Christmas Message,* 1949.

CHAPTER X

Remedies Which Further Aggravate the Contemporary Economic Disorder

99

Q. *Can recourse to free competition or to monopolies heal the inequalities characteristic of the contemporary economic disorder?*

A. Neither free competition nor, much less, monopolies can lead economic life to an order aiming at the good of the individual and the common **good.**

Pius XI: "Free competition, however, though within certain limits just and productive of good results, cannot be the ruling principle of the economic world. . . . Still less can this function be exercised by the economic dictatorship which in recent times has taken the place of free competition, for this is a headstrong and vehement power, which, if it is to prove beneficial to mankind, needs to be curbed strongly and ruled with prudence. It cannot, however, be curbed and governed by itself. More loftly and noble principles must therefore be sought in order to control this dictatorship sternly and uncompromisingly." *Quadragesimo anno,* p. 211, #88.

Pius XII: "The course of events has shown how deceitful is the illusion of entrusting peace to free exchange alone. Nor would the result be otherwise in the future if there were to persist that blind faith which confers on economics an imaginary mystic force." *Christmas Message,* 1954.

100

Q. *Can the good of the individual and of society be attained by an economic reorganization based on a materialistic concept of life?*

A. A system based on a materialistic concept of life, even when successful in increasing production, would fail to organize economic life properly, for it would do so at a great cost to the freedom and dignity of man.

PIUS XI: "Communism teaches and pursues a twofold aim: merciless class warfare and complete abolition of private ownership. . . . We do not think it necessary to warn . . . against the impious and nefarious character of Communism." *Quadragesimo anno,* pp. 218, 219, #112.

PIUS XI: "Communism, moreover, strips man of his liberty, robs human personality of all its dignity, and removes all the moral restraints that check the eruptions of blind impulse. There is no recognition of any right of the individual in his relations to the collectivity; no natural right is accorded to human personality, which is a mere cogwheel in the Communist system. In man's relations with other individuals, besides, Communists hold the principle of absolute equality. . . . What men call authority and subordination is derived from the community as its first and only font. Nor is the individual granted any property rights over material goods or the means of production, for inasmuch as these are the source of further wealth, their possession would give one man power over another. . . .

"Such a doctrine logically makes of marriage and the

family a purely artificial and civil institution. . . . There exists no matrimonial bond of a juridico-moral nature that is not subject to the whim of the individual or of the collectivity. Naturally, therefore, the notion of an indissoluble marriage tie is denied. Communism is particularly characterized by the rejection of any link that binds woman to the family and the home, and her emancipation is proclaimed as a basic principle. She is withdrawn from the family and the care of her children, to be thrust, instead, into public life and collective production under the same conditions as man. The care of home and children devolves upon the collectivity.

"Finally, the right of education is denied to parents, for it is conceived as the exclusive prerogative of the community, in whose name and by whose mandate alone parents may exercise this right." *Divini Redemptoris,* p. 345, #10 and 11.

Pius XI: "What would be the condition of a human society based on such materialistic tenets? It would be collectivity with no other hierarchy than that of the economic system. It would have only one mission: the production of material things by means of collective labor, so that the goods of this world might be enjoyed in a paradise where each would 'give according to his powers' and would 'receive according to his needs.'

"Communism recognizes in the collectivity the right, or rather, unlimited discretion, to draft individuals for the labor of the collectivity with no regard for their personal welfare; so that even violence could be legitimately exercised to dragoon the recalcitrant against their wills. In the Communistic commonwealth morality and law would be nothing but a derivation of the existing economic order, purely earthly in origin and unstable in character. In a word . . . 'humanity without God.'" *Divini Redemptoris,* p. 346, #11 and 12.

Pius XI: "The doctrine of modern Communism, which

is often concealed under the most seductive trappings, is in substance based on the principles of dialectical and historical materialism previously advocated by Marx, of which the theoreticians of Bolshevism claim to possess the only genuine interpretation. According to this doctrine, there is in the world only one reality, matter, the blind forces. . . . Even human society is nothing but a phenomenon and form of matter. . . . By a law of inexorable necessity and through a perpetual conflict of forces, matter moves toward the final synthesis of a classless society. In such a doctrine, as is evident, there is no room for the idea of God; there is no difference between matter and spirit, between soul and body; there is neither survival of the soul after death nor any hope in a future life. Insisting on the dialectical aspect of their materialism, the Communists claim that the conflict which carries the world toward its final synthesis can be accelerated by man. . . . Thus the class struggle . . . takes on the aspect of a crusade for the progress of humanity." *Divini Redemptoris*, p. 344, #9.

PIUS XI: "The Communism of today, more emphatically than similar movements in the past, conceals in itself a false messianic idea. A pseudo-ideal of justice, of equality and fraternity in labor impregnates all its doctrine and activity with a deceptive mysticism which communicates a zealous and contagious enthusiasm to the multitudes entrapped by delusive promises. This is especially true in an age like ours, when unusual misery has resulted from the unequal distribution of the goods of this world. This pseudo-ideal is even boastfully advanced as if it were responsible for a certain economic progress. As a matter of fact, when such progress is at all real, its true causes are quite different, as for instance, the intensification of industrialism in countries which were formerly almost without it, the exploitation of immense natural resources, and the use of the most brutal methods to insure the achievement of gigantic projects with a minimum of expense." *Divini Redemptoris,* p. 343, #8.

Pius XI: "Not only does [Socialism] condemn recourse to physical force; it even mitigates and moderates to some extent class warfare and the abolition of private property, if it does not reject them entirely. . . . It cannot be denied that its programs often strikingly approach the just demands of Christian social reformers. . . .

"We pronounce as follows: whether socialism be considered as a doctrine, or as a historical fact, or as a movement, if it really remain socialism it cannot be brought into harmony with the dogmas of the Catholic Church, even after it has yielded to truth and justice in the points We have mentioned; the reason being that it conceives human society in a way utterly alien to Christian truth. . . .

"Socialism, on the contrary, entirely ignorant of and unconcerned about this sublime end both of individuals and of society, affirms that human society was instituted merely for the sake of material advantages. . . .

"The socialists argue that economic production . . . must necessarily be carried on collectively, and that because of this necessity men must surrender and submit themselves wholly to society so far as the production of wealth is concerned. Indeed, the possession of the greatest possible amount of temporal goods is esteemed so highly that man's higher goods, not excepting liberty, must, they claim, be subordinated and even sacrificed to the exigencies of the most efficient production. . . . Society, therefore, as the socialist conceives it, is, on the one hand, impossible and unthinkable without the use of compulsion of the most excessive kind: on the other, it fosters a false liberty, since in such a scheme no place is found for true social authority, which is not based on temporal and material advantages, but descends from God alone, the Creator and last end of all things.

"If, like all errors, socialism contains a certain element of truth . . . it is nevertheless founded upon a doctrine of human society peculiarly its own, which is opposed to true Christianity." *Quadragesimo anno*, p. 219, #113; p. 221, #117–119; p. 222, #120.

Pius XI: "Communism is intrinsically wrong, and no one who would save Christian civilization may collaborate with it in any undertaking whatsoever. Those who permit themselves to be deceived into lending their aid toward the triumph of Communism in their own country, will be the first to fall victims of their error. And the greater the antiquity and grandeur of the Christian civilization in the regions where Communism successfully penetrates, so much more devastating will be the hatred displayed by the Godless." *Divini Redemptoris*, p. 365, #60.

Pius XII: "We reject Communism as a social system by virtue of Christian doctrine, and We have a particular obligation to proclaim the fundamental principles of natural law. For the same reasons We also reject the opinion that the Christian ought today to see Communism as a phenomenon or a stage in the passage of history, one of the necessary 'moments,' as it were, of its evolution, and consequently to accept it as if decreed by Divine Providence." *Christmas Message*, 1955.

101

Q. *Can a new social order be established separately from a religious and moral reform?*

A. Since the social element in man cannot be separated from the moral, so, too, the promoting of a new social order through social reforms apart from a reform of the moral and religious life of the individual and society is unthinkable, for the social and moral life are inseparable.

Pius XII: "Certain Catholics, promoters of a new social order, are in error when they maintain that social reform must come first of all and that afterwards care will be taken of the religious and moral life of the individual and society. The first cannot, in fact, be separated from the second, because this world cannot be disjoined from the other; nor can man, who is a living whole, be broken up into two parts." *Address to the Italian Catholic Workers Association*, May 14, 1953.

Pius XII: "We urge them to build up a society in which man's security rests on that moral order of which We have very often set forth the need and the consequences, and which has regard for true human nature." *Christmas Message*, 1955.

CHAPTER XI

The Church and the Reorganization of Economic Life

102

Q. *Does the Church have any criteria to offer toward the reorganization of economic life?*

A. The Church has neither the duty nor the means of suggesting a rationalizing system of the economic life, but she can and must (cf. Q. 82) indicate the ways by which, always respecting the divine natural and positive rights, economists and lawmakers can proceed toward an economic reorganization capable of bringing about the good of the individual and the material common good.

PIUS XI: "Even in the sphere of social economics, although the Church has never proposed a definite technical system, since this is not her field, she has nevertheless clearly outlined the guiding principles which, while susceptible of varied concrete applications according to the diversified conditions of times and places and peoples, indicate the safe way of securing the happy progress of society." *Divini Redemptoris*, p. 335, #33.

PIUS XII: "The Church does not restrict itself to demanding a social order of greater justice, but sets out its fundamental principles, urging the rulers of nations, legislators, employers and management to give them practical application." *Address to the Christian Labor Unions of Italy*, May 1, 1955.

103

Q. *What does the action of the Church in the economic field consist in?*

A. The action of the Church in the reorganizing of the economic life consists of: 1) stating and defending the limits of the natural and the divine-positive rights of the economic order; 2) suggesting those means which in the various historical situations may be more apt to favor the economic reorganization, with the good of the individual and the general common good in view; 3) attending to the improvements of morals without which any work of reorganization would be futile; 4) participating through its own institutions in the promotion and the practice of justice, charity and social harmony.

LEO XIII: "Doubtless this most serious question demands the attention and the efforts of others besides Ourselves. . . . But We affirm without hesitation that all the striving of men will be vain if they leave out the Church. It is the Church that proclaims from the Gospel those teachings by which the conflict can be brought to an end, or at least made far less bitter. The Church uses her efforts, not only to enlighten the mind, but to direct by her precepts the life and conduct of men. The Church improves and ameliorates the condition of the working man by numerous useful organizations. She, moreover, does her best to enlist the services of all ranks in discussing and endeavouring to meet, in the most practical way, the claims of the working classes; and she acts on the decided view that for these purposes recourse should be had, in due measure and degree, to the help of the law and of State authority. . . . But the Church is not content with pointing out the remedy. She also applies it. For the Church does her utmost to teach and train men and to educate them. . . . She strives to influence the mind and heart . . . that civil society may be renovated in every part by the teachings of Christianity. . . ." *Rerum novarum*, pp. 175–176, #13; p. 182, #22.

Leo XIII: "The Church . . . recognizes inequalities among men, who are born with different powers of body and mind, unequal in possession also, and holds that the right of property and of ownership . . . springs from nature itself. . . . But never, because of all this, does our holy Mother neglect the care of the poor. . . . Rather, drawing them to her with a mother's embrace . . . she holds them in great honour. She does all she can to help them; she provides homes and hospitals where they may be received, nourished, and cared for all the world over, and watches over these. She is constantly impressing on the rich that most grave precept to give to the poor what remains. . . . In fine, she does all she can to relieve and comfort the poor, either by holding up to them the example of Christ . . . or by reminding them of His own words, wherein He pronounced the poor blessed and bade them hope for the reward of eternal bliss." *Quod apostolici muneris*, p. 22, #9.

Pius XII: "The Church always takes the part of those who possess only their work by which to win their daily bread for themselves and their families. She always defends their just rights and reasonable demands." *Address to the Catholic Action Congress*, April 29, 1945.

104

Q. *What will happen if the findings and the counsels of the Church are disregarded?*

A. Disregarding the Church's findings and counsels concerning the reformation of economic life would hasten the subjection of the many to the few; and continuous unrest would interfere with the good of the individual and with the common good.

LEO XIII: "For, as the very evidence of facts and events shows, if this method is rejected or disregarded, one of two things must occur: either the greater portion of the human race will fall back into the vile condition of slavery which so long prevailed among the pagan nations, or human society must continue to be disturbed by constant eruptions, to be disgraced by rapine and strife. . . ." *Quod apostolici muneris,* p. 22, #9.

PIUS XI: "Nor is it lawful to fix such a scanty wage as will be insufficient for the upkeep of the family in the circumstances in which it is placed." *Casti connubii,* p. 169, #123.

CHAPTER XII

Natural Characteristics of the Economic Order

105

Q. *Can a reorganization of the economic life ignore the natural inequalities among men?*

A. Nature is responsible for the great diversity of talents among men, and therefore of their capacities, from which the individual as well as the community draw their benefits, and from which social inequalities are also derived. A reordaining of the economic life cannot ignore these factors, but rather should benefit by them.

LEO XIII: "Let it be laid down, in the first place, that humanity must remain as it is. It is impossible to reduce human society to a level. . . . All striving against nature is vain. There naturally exist among mankind innumerable differences of the most important kind. People differ in capability, in diligence, in health, and in strength; and thus inequality in fortune is a necessary result of inequality in condition. Such inequality is far from being disadvantageous either to individuals or to the community. Social and public life can only go on by the help of various kinds of capacity. . . ." *Rerum novarum,* p. 176, #14.

LEO XIII: "In accordance with the teachings of the Gospel, the equality of men consists in this: that all, having inherited the same nature, are called to the same most high dignity of the sons of God; and that, as one and the same end is set before all, each one is to be judged by the same law and will receive punishment or reward according to his deserts." *Quod apostolici muneris,* p. 18, #5.

Pius XII: "In a people worthy of the name, all inequalities based not on whim but on the nature of things, inequalities of culture, possessions, social standing— without, of course, prejudice to justice and mutual charity—do not constitute any obstacle to the existence and the prevalence of a true spirit of union and brotherhood." *Christmas Message,* 1944.

106

Q. *Is the right to private ownership a natural right?*

A. Man has a natural right to private ownership. This is a fitting reward for the industrious development of his personality, guarantees the free choice of the means (necessary and useful) for his own individual life and that of his family, stimulates production with benefit to the whole of society, and increases attachment to his place of birth.

Leo XIII: "For every man has by nature the right to possess property as his own. . . . And on this account— namely, that man alone among animals possesses reason —it must be within his right to have things not merely for temporary and momentary use, as other living beings have them, but in stable and permanent possession; he must have not only things which perish in the using, but also those which, though used, remain for use in the future. . . . For man comprehends by the power of his reason things innumerable, and joins the future with the present. Being, moreover, the master of his own acts, he governs himself by the foresight of his counsel, under the eternal law and the power of God, whose Providence governs all things. Wherefore, it is in his power to exercise his choice not only on things which regard his present welfare, but also on those which will be for his advantage in time to come. Hence man can possess not only the fruits of the earth, but also the earth itself; for of the products of the earth he can make provision for the future. Man's needs do not die out, but recur; satisfied today, they demand new supplies tomorrow. Nature, therefore, owes to man a storehouse that shall never fail, the daily supply of his daily wants. And this he finds only in the inexhaustible fertility of the earth.

"Nor must we, at this stage, have recourse to the State. Man is older than the State and he holds the right of providing for the life of his body prior to the formation of any State. . . .

"Now, when man thus spends the industry of his mind and the strength of his body in procuring the fruits of nature, by that act he makes his own that portion of nature's field which he cultivates—that portion on which he leaves, as it were, the impress of his own personality; and it cannot but be just that he should possess that portion as his own, and should have a right to keep it without molestation." *Rerum novarum*, pp. 170–172 *passim*.

PIUS XI: "The right to own private property has been given to man by nature or rather by the Creator Himself, not only in order that individuals may be able to provide for their own needs and those of their families, but also that by means of it, the goods which the Creator has destined for the human race may truly serve this purpose." *Quadragesimo anno*, p. 193, #45.

PIUS XII: "The dignity of the human person, then, requires normally as a natural foundation of life the right to the use of the goods of the earth. To this right corresponds the fundamental obligation to grant private ownership of property, if possible, to all." *Christmas Message*, 1942.

LEO XIII: "Men always work harder and more readily when they work on that which is their own; nay, they learn to love the very soil which yields in response to the labour of their hands, not only food to eat, but an abundance of good things for themselves and those that are dear to them. It is evident how such a spirit of willing labour would add to the produce of the earth and to the wealth of the community. A third advantage still would arise from the fact that men would cling to the country in which they were born." *Rerum novarum*, p. 195, #35.

PIUS XII: "Though with necessary adjustments to the times, family and property must remain among the fundamentals of the free settlement of persons." *Christmas Message*, 1955.

107

Q. *What is the end of labour?*

A. The immediate end of labor is the gaining of goods to hold and to use as private property.

LEO XIII: "It is surely undeniable that when a man engages in remunerative labour the very reason and motive of his work is to obtain property, and to hold it as his own private possession. If one hires out to another his strength or his industry, he does this for the purpose of receiving in return what is necessary for food and living; he thereby expressly proposes to acquire a full and real right, not only to the remuneration. . . . Thus, if he lives sparingly, saves money, and invests his savings, for greater security, in land, the land in such a case is only his wages in another form; and, consequently, a workingman's little estate thus purchased should be as completely at his own disposal as the wages he receives for his labour." *Rerum novarum,* p. 169, #4.

108

Q. *Is the right of hereditary transmission of one's goods inherent to the natural right of ownership?*

A. The right to the hereditary transmission of one's goods is part of the natural right of ownership.

Leo XIII: "Hence, the right of property, which has been proved to belong naturally to individual persons, must also belong to a man in his capacity of head of a family. Nay, such a person must possess this right so much the more clearly in proportion as his position multiplies his duties. For it is a most sacred law of nature that a father must provide food and all necessaries for those whom he has begotten. And, similarly, nature dictates that a man's children, who carry on, as it were, and continue his own personality, should be provided by him with all that is needful to enable them honourably to keep themselves from want and misery in the uncertainties of this mortal life. Now, in no other way can a father effect this except by the ownership of productive property [*fructuosarum possesione rerum*], which he can transmit to his children by inheritance." *Rerum novarum,* p. 173, #9 and 10.

109

Q. *Is the content of the natural right of ownership the same with all the various peoples?*

A. The discipline of gain, use and transfer even of the hereditary title to property is something which nature left free to the various peoples to regulate, so that without destroying it they may adapt it to the mutable requirement of the common good.

LEO XIII: "God has granted . . . that the limits of private possession have been left to be fixed by man's own industry and the laws of individual peoples." *Rerum novarum*, p. 171, #7.

PIUS XII: "Positive legislation regulating private ownership may change and more or less restrict its use." *Christmas Message*, 1942.

PIUS XII: "Every man, as a living being gifted with reason, has in fact from nature the fundamental right to make use of the material goods of the earth, while it is left to the will of man and to the juridical statutes of nations to regulate in greater detail the actuation of this right. This individual right cannot in any way be suppressed even by other clear and undisputed rights over material goods. Undoubtedly, the natural order, deriving from God, demands also private property and the free reciprocal commerce of goods by interchange and gift, as well as the functioning of the State as a control over both these institutions. But all this remains subordinated to the natural scope of material goods and cannot emancipate itself from the first and fundamental right which concedes their use to all men; but it should rather serve to make possible the actuation of this right in conformity with its scope. Only thus can we and must we secure that private property and the use of material goods bring to society peace and prosperity and long life, that they no longer set up precarious conditions which will give rise to struggles and jealousies, and which are left to the mercy of the blind interplay of force and weakness.

"The native right to the use of material goods, intimately

linked as it is to the dignity and other rights of the human person, together with the statutes mentioned above, provides man with a secure material basis of the highest import, on which to rise to the fulfillment, with reasonable liberty, of his moral duties. The safe guardianship of this right will ensure the personal dignity of man, and will facilitate for him the attention to and fulfillment of that sum of stable duties and decisions for which he is directly responsible to his Creator." *Address on Pentecost*, 1940.

PIUS XII: "Whosoever is not ready to limit justly in relation to the common weal the use of his private goods, be it done freely according to the dictates of his own conscience or even done by means of organized provisions of a public character, is helping, insofar as it depends on him, to impede the indispensable primacy of personal impulse and responsibility in social life." *Christmas Message*, 1954.

110

Q. *Does ownership have a social function?*

A. In view of the original destination of goods to common use, the owner must use for the benefit of the community that which exceeds his own needs, either by making work available or by supplying assistance to the needy.

PIUS XI: "At the same time a man's superfluous income is not left entirely to his own discretion. We speak of that portion of his income which he does not need in order to live as becomes his station. On the contrary, the grave obligations of charity, beneficence, and liberality which rest upon the wealthy are constantly insisted upon in telling words by Holy Scripture and the Fathers of the Church. However, according to the teaching of the Angelic Doctor, the investment of a large income in such a manner that favourable opportunities for employment may abound (on the supposition that the labor employed produces results which are really useful) is to be considered an act of real liberality and particularly appropriate to the needs of our time." *Quadragesimo anno*, p. 196, #50 and 51.

LEO XIII: "But if the question be asked, 'How must one's possessions be used?' the Church replies without hesitation in the words of the same holy Doctor: 'Man should not consider his outward possessions as his own, but as common to all, so as to share them without difficulty when others are in need.' . . . True, no one is commanded to distribute to others that which is required for his own necessities and those of his household; nor even to give away what is reasonably required to keep up becomingly his condition of life, 'for no one ought to live unbecomingly.' But when necessity has been supplied, and one's position fairly considered, it is a duty to give to the indigent out of that which is over. . . . It is a duty, not of justice (except in extreme cases), but of Christian charity—a duty which is not enforced by human law. . . . Thus to sum up what has been said: Whoever has received from the divine bounty a large share of blessings, whether they be external and corporal, or gifts of the mind, has received them for the purpose of using them for perfecting his own nature, and, at the same time, that he may employ them, as the minister of God's Providence, for the benefit of others." *Rerum novarum*, p. 180, #19.

111

Q. *Does one lose the right of ownership by the bad use of property?*

A. Since the right of ownership is something different from its use, they are not governed by the same principles. Therefore, the right of ownership is not lost for the abuse or non-use of it.

Pius XII: "Solidarity of men with each other demands, not only in the name of brotherly love but even of mutual advantage, that everything possible be done to maintain and increase employment. Therefore let those who are able to invest capital consider in the light of the common good, and with due regard to their economic condition, to the risks involved and the opportunity offered, whether they can reconcile with their conscience their neglect and failure to make investments because of unreasonable caution. On the other hand, those employers act against conscience who, by exploiting their own private business for selfish ends, prevent others from finding employment. And where private initiative is inactive or inadequate, the public authorities are obliged to provide employment, as far as possible, by undertaking works of general utility, and to facilitate by counseling and other means the finding of employment for those who seek it." *Christmas Message*, 1952.

Pius XI: "The right of property must be distinguished from its use. It belongs to what is called commutative justice, faithfully to respect the possessions of others, and not to encroach on the rights of another by exceeding one's own rights of ownership. The putting of one's own possessions to proper use, however, does not fall under this form of justice, but under certain other virtues, and therefore it is a duty which is not enforced by human laws. Hence it is false to contend that the right of ownership and its proper use are bounded by the same limits; and it is even less true that the very misuse or even the non-use of ownership destroys or forfeits the right to it." *Quadragesimo anno*, p. 194, #47.

Q. *What must be man's attitude with regard to riches?*

A. In view of man's end, riches are but means to be properly used, from which both the ones that have them and those who have not must be detached.

Leo XIII: "Money and the other things which men call good and desirable—we may have them in abundance or we may want them altogether; as far as eternal happiness is concerned, it does not matter. The only thing that is important is to use them rightly. . . . Therefore, those whom fortune favours are warned that freedom from sorrow and abundance of earthly riches, are no guarantee of that beatitude that shall never end, but rather the contrary (Matt. 19:23–24); that the rich should tremble at the threatenings of Jesus Christ, threatenings so strange in the mouth of Our Lord (Luke 6:24–25); and that a most strict account must be given to the Supreme Judge for all that we possess." *Rerum novarum*, p. 179, #18.

Pius XI: "The rich should not place their happiness in the things of earth nor spend their best efforts in the acquisition of them. Rather, considering themselves only as stewards of their earthly goods, let them be mindful of the account they must render of them to their Lord and Master and value them as precious means that God has put into their hands for doing good; let them not fail, besides, to distribute of their abundance to the poor, according to the evangelical precept. . . .

"But the poor too, in their turn, while engaged, according to the laws of charity and justice in acquiring the necessities of life and also in bettering their condition, should always remain 'poor in spirit,' and hold spiritual goods in higher esteem than earthly property and pleasures. Let them remember that the world will never be able to rid itself of misery, sorrow, and tribulation, which are the portion even of those who seem most prosperous. Patience, therefore, is the need of all." *Divini Redemptoris*, p. 359, #44 and 45.

113

Q. *Is there an insurmountable conflict between the rich and the poor, and capital and labour?*

A. The conflict existing between capital and labor, because of the selfishness of the capitalists and some demands by the proletariate, is unnatural. It can and must be resolved for the benefit of the two groups as well as of all society.

LEO XIII: "The great mistake that is made in the matter now under consideration, is to possess oneself of the idea that class is naturally hostile to class; that rich and poor are intended by nature to live at war with one another. . . . In a State it is ordained by nature that these two classes should exist in harmony and agreement, and should, as it were, fit into one another, so as to maintain the equilibrium of the body politic." *Rerum novarum*, p. 177, #15.

LEO XIII: "Capital cannot do without labour, nor labour without capital." *Rerum novarum*, p. 177, #15.

PIUS XI: "Hence it follows that unless a man apply his labour to his own property, an alliance must be formed between his toil and his neighbor's property, for each is helpless without the other. . . . It is therefore entirely false to ascribe the results of their combined efforts to either party alone; and it is flagrantly unjust that either should deny the efficacy of the other and claim the entire product.

"Property, in the sense of capital, however, was long able to appropriate to itself excessive advantages. . . . The cause of the harassed working man was espoused by the 'intellectuals,' as they are called, who set up in opposition to this fictitious law another equally false moral principle: that all products and profits, excepting those required to repair and replace invested capital, belong by every right to the working man. . . .

"Wealth . . . must be so distributed among the various individuals and classes of society that the common good of all . . . be thereby promoted. . . . By these principles of social justice one class is forbidden to exclude the other from a share in the profits. This sacred law is violated by a wealthy class who, as it were, carefree in their possessions, deem it a just state of things that they should receive everything and the labourer nothing. It is violated also by a propertyless wage-earning class who demand for themselves all the fruits of production, as being the work of their hands. Such men, vehemently incensed against the violation of justice by capitalists, go too far in vindicating the one right of which they are conscious; they attack and seek to abolish all forms of ownership and all income not obtained by labour, whatever be the nature or function these represent in human society, for the sole reason that they are not acquired by toil. . . . Each one, then, must receive his due share, and the distribution of created goods must be brought into conformity with the demands of the common good, that is, of social justice." *Quadragesimo anno*, p. 197, #53–54; p. 198, #55, 57–58.

114

Q. *What are the duties in justice of capitalist employers toward employees and of employees toward their capitalist employers?*

A. Capitalist employers must respect in their employees the dignity of the human person, their religious, spiritual and family needs, the limitation of their strength, their desire to save, their demand for a just wage. Employees in turn must faithfully perform their work freely agreed upon, respect the person and the property of their employers, vindicate by legitimate means their own rights, without allowing themselves to be swayed by a propaganda promising unreasonable and unjust reforms.

LEO XIII: "Religion teaches the rich man and the employer that their working people are not their slaves; that they must respect in every man his dignity as a man and as a Christian. . . . Thus, again, religion teaches that, as among the workmen's concerns are religion herself, and things spiritual and mental, the employer is bound to see that his employee has time for the duties of piety; that he be not exposed to corrupting influences and dangerous occasions; and that he be not led away to neglect his home and family or to squander his wages. Furthermore, the employer must never tax his working people beyond their strength, nor employ them in work unsuited to their sex or age. The employer's great and principal obligation is to give to everyone that which is just. To defraud anyone of wages that are his due is a crime which cries to the avenging anger of heaven. . . .

"Finally, the rich must religiously refrain from cutting down the workman's earnings, either by force, fraud, or by usurious dealing; and that with the more reason because the poor man is weak and unprotected, and because his slender means should be sacred in proportion to their scantiness." *Rerum novarum*, p. 178, #16 and 17.

LEO XIII: "Thus religion teaches the labouring man and the workman to carry out honestly and well all equitable agreements freely made, never to injure capital, nor to outrage the person of an employer; never to employ violence in representing his own cause, nor to engage in riot or disorder; and to have nothing to do with men of evil principles, who work upon the people with artful promises, and raise foolish hopes which usually end in disaster and in repentance when too late." *Rerum novarum*, p. 177, #16.

115

Q. *What is the purpose of organized labour?*

A.   The aim of lawfully organized labour is to protect the worker's rights, to improve by all morally lawful means his living conditions, to contribute to the construction of an order in which material prosperity is the resultant of a common sincere effort in promoting the welfare of society, in upholding the highest cultural values and those which flow from an indefectible union of minds and spirits.

Pius XII: "It is a mistake to think that the interests of the workers are served by the old methods of class warfare." *Address to Italian Workers*, May 1, 1953.

Pius XII: "The labour movement cannot rest content with material success, with a more perfect system of guarantees and assurances or with a greater measure of influence on the economic system. It cannot visualize its future in terms of opposition to other social classes or of the excessive ascendancy of the state over the individual. The goal it pursues must be sought in a social order where material prosperity is the result of the sincere collaboration of all for the welfare of all and serves as a support for the higher values of culture and, above all, for the indissoluble union of minds and hearts." *Address to Members of the Administrative Council of International Labor Organizations,* November 20, 1954, quoted in *The Pope Speaks.*

Pius XII: "No true Christian can find fault if you unite in strong organizations to defend your rights—while remaining aware of your duties—and to arrive at an improvement in your conditions of life. . . . You are therefore acting in full conformity with the Church's social teaching when, by all means permissible, you vindicate your just rights." *Address to Railroad Workers of Rome,* June 26, 1955.

116

Q. *Is the wage contract by its very nature unjust?*

A. The wage contract is not by its very nature unjust. However, it would favour the obtaining of the common good if the wage contract could be modified somewhat by a contract of partnership by which the wage-earners would share in the ownership, the management or the profits.

Pius XI: "Those who hold that the wage contract is essentially unjust, and that in its place must be introduced the contract of partnership, are certainly in error. . . . In the present state of human society, however, We deem it advisable that the wage contract should, when possible, be modified somewhat by a contract of partnership, as is already being tried in various ways to the not small gain both of the wage earners and of the employers. In this way workers and officials are made sharers in the ownership or the management or in some way participate in the profits." *Quadragesimo anno,* p. 201, #64; p. 202, #65.

117

Q. *What are the characteristics of a just wage?*

A. Since work is personal and necessary, and since the common good must be taken into account in remunerating labour, the wage 1) must be sufficient for the wage-earner's personal and family needs; 2) must take into account the economic status of the plant; 3) must harmonize with the general economic well-being.

LEO XIII: "Doubtless before we can decide whether wages are equitable many things have to be considered." *Rerum novarum,* p. 178, #17.

LEO XIII: "Wages, we are told, are fixed by free consent. . . . The only way, it is said, in which injustice could happen, would be if the master refused to pay the whole of the wages, or the workman would not complete the work undertaken; when this happens the State should intervene to see that each obtains his own, but not under any other circumstances. This mode of reasoning is by no means convincing to a fair-minded man, for there are important considerations which it leaves out of view altogether. To labour is to exert one's self for the sake of procuring what is necessary for the purposes of life, and most of all for self-preservation. . . . Therefore, a man's labour has two notes or characters. First, of all, it is *personal;* for the exertion of individual power belongs to the individual. . . . Secondly, a man's labour is *necessary;* for without the results of labour a man cannot live; and self-conservation is a law of nature, which it is wrong to disobey. Now, if we were to consider labour merely so far as it is *personal,* doubtless it would be within the workman's right to accept any rate of wages whatever. . . . The labour of the working man is not only his personal attribute, but is *necessary.* . . . Let it be granted, then, that, as a rule, workman and employer should make free agreements, and in particular should freely agree as to wages; . . . the remuneration must be enough to support the wage earner in reasonable and frugal comfort. If through necessity . . . the workman accepts harder conditions he is the victim of force and injustice." *Rerum novarum,* pp. 192 and 193, #34.

Pius XI: "In estimating a just wage, not one consideration alone but many must be taken into account.

"In the first place, the wage paid to the workingman must be sufficient for the support of himself and of his family. . . .

"The condition of any particular business and of its owner must also come into question in settling the scale of wages; for it is unjust to demand wages so high that an employer cannot pay them without ruin, and without consequent distress among the working people themselves. . . .

"Finally, the wage scale must be regulated with a view to the economic welfare of the whole people. . . .

"To lower or raise wages unduly, with a view to private profit, and with no consideration for the common good, is contrary to social justice. . . ." *Quadragesimo anno,* p. 202, #66; p. 203, #71 and 72; p. 204, #74.

118

Q. *What is the purpose of the economic activity of a people?*

A. The primary end of the economic activity of a people is to assure the permanent material conditions favourable to the full development of the personality of each individual citizen. An abundant production will not fulfill this purpose unless it is reasonably distributed.

Pius XI: "For then only will the economic and social order be soundly established and attain its end, when it secures for all and each those goods which the wealth and resources of nature, technical achievement, and the social constitution of economic affairs can give. These goods should be sufficient to supply all needs and an honest livelihood, and to uplift men to that higher level of prosperity and culture which, provided it be used with prudence, is not only no hindrance but is of singular help to virtue." *Quadragesimo anno*, p. 205, #75.

Pius XII: "The national economy, as it is the product of the men who work together in the community of the State, has no other end than to secure without interruption the material conditions in which the individual life of the citizens may fully develop. . . . The economic riches of a people do not properly consist in the abundance of goods . . . but in the fact that such an abundance represents and offers really and effectively the material basis sufficient for the proper personal development of its members. If such a just distribution of goods were not secure or were effected only imperfectly, the real scope of national economy would not be attained." *Message on Pentecost*, 1941.

Pius XII: "It seems, therefore, that efforts must be made to attain the highest possible level of employment, but at the same time that means must be sought to ensure its stability." *Christmas Message*, 1952.

119

Q. *Can the rationalization of economic life take place spontaneously?*

A. The rationalization of economic life cannot be left to free competition. After bringing free competition within just and reasonable limits, there is need of the intervention of a public authority guided by the principles of social justice and charity in order that the common good may be attained.

Pius XI: "The proper ordering of economic affairs cannot be left to free competition alone. . . . It is therefore very necessary that economic affairs be once more subjected to and governed by a true and effective guiding principle. . . . More lofty and noble principles must therefore be sought in order to control this dictatorship sternly and uncompromisingly: to wit, social justice and social charity.

"To that end all the institutions of public and social life must be imbued with the spirit of justice, and this justice must above all be truly operative. It must build up a juridical and social order able to pervade all economic activity. Social charity should be, as it were, the soul of this order, and the duty of the state will be with promptness to protect and to defend it effectively." *Quadragesimo anno*, pp. 211–212, #88.

Pius XI: "Since the present economic regime is based mainly upon capital and labour, it follows that the principles of right reason or Christian social philosophy regarding capital, labour, and their mutual cooperation must be accepted in theory and reduced to practice. . . . The mutual relations between capital and labour must be determined according to the laws of the strictest justice, called commutative justice, supported however by Christian charity. Free competition, kept within just and definite limits, and still more economic domination, must be brought under the effective control of the public authority, in matters appertaining to this latter's competence. The public institutions of the nations must be such as to make the whole of human society conform to the common good, that is, to the standard of social justice." *Quadragesimo anno*, pp. 217–218, #110.

Pius XII: "Economic life means social life. The essential scope of the former—to which individuals are equally bound to help in the different spheres of their activity—is to assure in a stable manner for all members of society the material conditions required for the development of cultural and spiritual life. But satisfactory results are not possible apart from an external order and social norms which aim at lasting achievement of this objective. An appeal to an automatic and magic law is a mirage, no less vain in the economic order than in any other sphere of human activity." *Address to Members of the International Trade Convention,* March 7, 1948.

Counsels of the Church for the Reforming of Institutions and Practices in the Economic Field

---

120

Q. *What is needed for a rationalization of economic life for its human ends?*

A. The rationalization of economic life for human purposes demands a moral renewal and the reforming of institutions.

Pius XI: For the restoration of the social order "two things are particularly necessary: the reform of institutions and moral betterment." *Quadragesimo anno*, p. 206, #77.

121

Q. *Does the reorganization of economic life require the rejection of technical progress?*

A. The reorganization of economic life does not require a renunciation of technical progress; on the contrary, with due protection of the rights of man, such renunciation is to be condemned, since technical progress is a useful instrument for the betterment of man's lot.

Pius XII: "From our words directed against the materialism of the past century and of the present time, it would be wrong to deduce a condemnation of technical progress. No, we do not condemn that which is a gift of God." *Christmas Message,* 1941.

Pius XII: "The Church desires that certain limitations be placed upon the loss which modern man has experienced as the result of the predominance of mechanized progress and the ever increasing development of mechanical industry." *Address to Italian Workers,* October 20, 1947.

Pius XII: "Whoever, therefore, would furnish assistance to the needs of individuals and peoples cannot rely upon the security of an impersonal system of men and matter, no matter how vigorously developed in its technical aspects. Every plan or program must be inspired by the principle that man, as subject, guardian, and promoter of human values is more important than mere things, is more important than the practical applications of scientific progress, and that above all it is imperative to preserve from unwholesome depersonalization the essential forms of the social order and to use them to create and develop human relationships. If the forces of society are aimed at this end, they will not only realize one of their natural functions, but they will help greatly to relieve the necessities of the moment. For the forces of society have the task of encouraging full and reciprocal solidarity among individuals and among peoples." *Christmas Message,* 1952.

Pius XII: "Wealth and labour, the projects and inventions, the boasts and torments of our modern age must be considered in relation to man, the image of God." *Christmas Message,* 1955.

122

Q. *Who must attend to the reforming of institutions?*

A. The reforming of institutions for the reordering of economic life must be attended to by the

State in each individual country, in harmony with its minor societies. In the international field it must proceed from agreements between States.

PIUS XI: "When We speak of the reform of institutions it is primarily the State we have in mind. Not, indeed, as if we were to look for all salvation from its intervention, but because on account of the evil of Individualism, as we call it, things have come to such a pass that the highly developed social life which once flourished in a variety of prosperous institutions, organically linked with one another, has been laid prostrate and all but ruined, leaving thus virtually only individuals and the State. . . .

"The aim of social policy must therefore be the reestablishment of 'Orders' . . . in which men are knit together, not according to the position they occupy in the labour market, but according to the diverse functions which they exercise in society. For it is natural for those . . . who practice the same trade or profession, economic or otherwise, to combine into guilds or corporate groups [*collegia seu corpora*]. These organizations, in a true sense autonomous, are considered by man to be, if not essential to civil society, at least natural to it. . . . The proper ordering of economic affairs cannot be left to free competition alone. . . . It is therefore very necessary that economic affairs be once more subjected to and governed by a true and effective guiding principle . . . social justice and social charity. . . . It would be well if the various nations . . . strove to promote a healthy economic cooperation by prudent pacts and institutions." *Quadragesimo anno,* pp. 206–212 *passim.*

123

Q. *How will the State attend to the reorganization of economic life?*

A. The State will attend to the reorganization of economic life primarily by an appropriate and wise general administration, and by correcting the weaknesses of the economic activities of private individuals and their associations.

Leo XIII: "The first duty, therefore, of the rulers of the State should be to make sure that the laws and institutions, the general character and administration of the commonwealth, shall be such as to produce of themselves public well-being and private prosperity." *Rerum novarum,* p. 185, #26.

Pius XI: "The State itself, mindful of its responsibility before God and society, should be a model of prudence and sobriety in the administration of the commonwealth. Today more than ever the acute world crisis demands that those who dispose of immense funds, built up on the sweat and toil of millions, keep constantly and singly in mind the common good." *Divini Redemptoris,* p. 372, #81.

Leo XIII: "Whenever the general interest of any particular class suffers, or is threatened with evils which can in no other way be met, the public authority must step in to meet them." *Rerum novarum,* p. 188, # 28.

124

Q. *May the State intervene to regulate and promote production?*

A. The right and the duty to promote productive activity rests with employers and employees. However, if they should fail to produce in a way that is consonant with the common good, the State has the duty to intervene, taking care to respect in a general way the individual character of labour and consequently all the natural rights of the human person.

PIUS XII: "The duty and the right to organize the labour of the people belongs above all to the people immediately interested: the employers and the workers. If they do not fulfill their functions or cannot because of particular extraordinary contingencies fulfill them, then it falls back on the State to intervene in the field of labour and in the division and distribution of work according to the form and measure that the common good properly understood demands.

"In any case, every legitimate and beneficial interference of the State in the field of labour should be such as to safeguard and respect its personal character, both in the broad outlines and, as far as possible, in what concerns its execution; and this will happen if the norms of the State do not abolish or render impossible the exercise of other rights and duties equally personal." *Message on Pentecost,* 1941.

PIUS XI: "The State must take every measure necessary to supply employment, particularly for the heads of families and for the young. To achieve this end demanded by the pressing needs of the common welfare, the wealthy classes must be induced to assume those burdens without which human society cannot be saved nor they themselves remain secure. However, measures taken by the State with this end in view ought to be such that they will strike at those who hold in their hands too great a share of capital and who continue augmenting it with serious injury to others." *Divini Redemptoris,* p. 372, #81.

PIUS XII: "To make of this state enterprise the normal rule for public economic organization would mean reversing the order of things." *Address to Catholic Employers,* March 7, 1949.

Pius XII: "One of the essential points of Christian social doctrine has always been the affirmation of the primary importance of private enterprise as compared to the subsidiary function of state enterprise. This is not to deny the usefulness and the necessity, in some cases, of government intervention, but rather to bring out this truth: that the human person not only represents the purpose of the economy, but is its most important element." *Address to the Christian Employers' Association of Italy, June 6, 1955.*

125

Q. *Does the reform of institutions include also the reform of the right of private ownership?*

A. The State must respect man's natural right to private ownership; moreover, in the present circumstances the State can and must endeavour to make it possible for all; it must also regulate its use so as to harmonize it with the common good.

Leo XIII: "The right to possess private property is from nature, not from man; and the State has only the right to regulate its use in the interests of the public good, but by no means to abolish it altogether." *Rerum novarum,* p. 195, #35.

Leo XIII: "We have seen that this great labour question cannot be solved except by assuming as a principle that private ownership must be held sacred and inviolable. The law, therefore, should favour ownership, and its policy should be to induce as many people as possible to become owners. . . . If working people can be encouraged to look forward to obtaining a share in the land, the result will be that the gulf between vast wealth and deep poverty will be bridged over, and the two orders will be brought nearer together." *Rerum novarum,* p. 194, #35.

Pius XI: "It follows from the twofold character of ownership, which We have termed individual and social, that men must take into account in this matter not only their own advantage but also the common good. To define in detail these duties, when the need occurs and when the natural law does not do so, is the function of the government. Provided that the natural and divine law be observed, the public authority, in view of the true necessity of the common good, may specify more accurately what is licit and what is illicit for property owners in the use of their possessions. Moreover, Leo XIII had wisely taught that 'the limits of private possession have been left to be fixed by man's own industry and the laws of individual peoples.'

"It is plain, however, that the State may not discharge this duty in an arbitrary manner. Man's natural right of privately possessing and transmitting property by inheritance must be kept intact and cannot be taken away by the State, 'for man is older than the State' and 'the domestic household is anterior both in idea and in fact to the gathering of men into a commonwealth.' Hence the prudent Pontiff had already declared it unlawful for the State to exhaust the means of individuals by crushing taxes and tributes." *Quadragesimo anno,* pp. 194–195, #49.

Pius XII: "The dignity of the human person, then, requires normally as a natural foundation of life the right to the use of the goods of the earth. To this right corresponds the fundamental obligation to grant private ownership of property, if possible, to all. Positive legislation regulating private ownership may change and more or less restrict its use. But if legislation is to play its part in the pacification of the community, it must prevent the worker who is or will be a father of a family, from being condemned to an economic dependence and slavery which is irreconcilable with his rights as a person. Whether this slavery arises from the exploitation of private capital or from the power of the State, the result is the same. Indeed, under the pressure of a State which dominates all and controls the whole field of public and private life, even going into the realm of ideas and beliefs and of conscience, the lack of liberty can have the most serious consequences, as experience shows and proves." *Christmas Message, 1942.*

126

Q. *May the ownership of certain goods be assigned to the collectivity?*

A. When private ownership of certain goods constitutes a danger to the common good, it can be assigned to the community, for the attainment of the common good would require just that.

PIUS XI: "For it is rightly contended that certain forms of property must be reserved to the State, since they carry with them an opportunity of domination too great to be left to private individuals without injury to the community at large." *Quadragesimo anno,* p. 220, #114.

127

Q. *Is the socialization of business enterprises to be permitted?*

A. The socialization of business enterprises is permissible upon due compensation, if this is demanded by the common good or is necessary to remedy some abuse or to avoid waste and assure an organic marshalling of the productive forces.

Pius XII: "The Catholic Associations support socialization only in cases where it appears really necessary for the common welfare; in other words, when it is the only means to remedy an injustice and to ensure the co-ordinated use of the same forces to the benefit of the economic life of the nation, so that the normal and peaceful development of the economic life may open the gates to material prosperity which may become a sound foundation for the development of cultural and religious life. In any case, the Associations recognize that socialization carries with it the obligation of fitting compensation such as in concrete circumstances is just and fair to those concerned." *Address to the Catholic Workers' Association*, March 11, 1945.

128

Q. *Is the State's intervention in the matter of the distribution of wealth necessary and effective?*

A. By means of appropriate provisions the State must prevent the accumulation of wealth in the hands of the few and favour a generous distribution of the accumulated wealth among wage earners.

Pius XI: "Every effort, therefore, must be made that at least in future a just share only of the fruits of production be permitted to accumulate in the hands of the wealthy, and an ample sufficiency be supplied to the workingmen. The purpose is not that these become slack at their work . . . but that by thrift they may increase their possessions and by the prudent management of the same may be enabled to bear the family burden with greater ease and security, being freed from that hand-to-mouth uncertainty which is the lot of the proletarian. Thus they will not only be in a position to support life's changing fortunes, but will also have the reassuring confidence that when their lives are ended, some little provision will remain for those whom they leave behind them." *Quadragesimo anno*, p. 201, #61.

Pius XII: "The natural course of affairs, no doubt, brings with it, within certain limits—this is neither economically nor socially abnormal—an unequal distribution of the goods of the world. But the Church is opposed to the accumulation of these goods in the hands of relatively small and exceedingly rich groups, while vast masses of people are condemned to pauperism and to an economic condition unworthy of human beings." *Address to Catholic Men*, Sept. 9, 1947.

Pius XII: "It is upon the basis of this solidarity, and not upon worthless and unstable systems, that we call upon men to build the social fabric. Solidarity demands that outrageous and provoking inequalities in living standards among different groups in a nation be eliminated. To achieve this urgent end the efficacious voice of conscience is preferable to external compulsion. Conscience will know how to set limits to expenditures for luxuries and likewise persuade those of more modest means to provide before all else for what is necessary and useful, and then to save whatever is left over." *Christmas Message*, 1952.

Pius XII: "It is not a question today of merely distributing the products of the social economy more equitably in closer correspondence with the labour and the needs of individuals. . . . Under present conditions . . . every social reform is strictly bound up with the question of a prudent organization of production . . . for it is clear that there can never be sufficient distribution where there is not sufficient production. . . . But if this productivity is attained as a result of unbridled competition and of an unprincipled expenditure of wealth, or by oppression and despotic exploitation of labour and the needs of individuals on the part of the State, it cannot be sound and natural, because social economy is an organizing of workers, and every worker is endowed with human dignity and freedom. The immoderate exploitation of genuine human values . . . leads sooner or later to decadence." *Address to the Sacred College,* June 2, 1948.

129

Q. *Should the State show any particular interest in the working class?*

A. In view of their conditions and number, of their contribution to social prosperity, their rights as individuals and the common good, the State owes the working class particular consideration; hence, it must protect their spiritual, physical and economic needs, and favour the development of their personality.

LEO XIII: "The poor are members of the national community equally with the rich; they are real component parts, living parts, which make up, through the family, the living body; and it need hardly be said that they are by far the majority. It would be irrational to neglect one portion of the citizens and to favour another; and therefore the public administration must duly and solicitously provide for the welfare and the comfort of the working people, or else that law of justice will be violated which ordains that each shall have his due." *Rerum novarum,* p. 186, #27.

"In all well-constituted States it is by no means an unimportant matter to provide those bodily and external commodities 'the use of which is necessary to virtuous action.' And in the provision of material well-being, the labour of the poor—the exercise of their skill and the employment of their strength in the culture of the land and the workshops of trade—is most efficacious and altogether indispensable. Indeed, their cooperation in this respect is so important that *it may truly be said that it is only by the labour of the workingman that States grow rich.*

"Justice, therefore, demands that the interests of the poorer population be carefully watched over by the Administration, so that they who contribute so largely to the advantage of the community may themselves share in the benefits they create—that being housed, clothed, and enabled to support life, they may find their existence less hard and more endurable. *It follows that whatever shall appear to be conducive to the well-being of those who work, should receive favourable consideration.* Let it not be feared that solicitude of this kind will injure any interest. On the contrary, it will be to the advantage of all; for it cannot but be good for the commonwealth to secure from misery those on whom it so largely depends." *Op. cit.*, p. 187, #27.

"Those who are badly off have no resources of their own to fall back upon, and must chiefly rely upon the assistance of the State. And it is for this reason that wage-earners, who are, undoubtedly, among the weak and necessitous, should be specially cared for and protected by the commonwealth." *Ibid.*, p. 189, #29.

"The workman, too, has property and possessions in which he must be protected; and, first of all, there are his spiritual and mental interests. . . . From this follows the obligation of the cessation of work and labour on Sundays and certain festivals. . . . If we turn now to things exterior and corporal, the first concern of all is to save the poor workers from the cruelty of grasping men who use human beings as mere instruments for making money." *Ibid.*, p. 190, #32; p. 191, #33.

"If circumstances were such that among the labouring population the ties of family life were relaxed; if religion were found to suffer through the workmen not having time and opportunity to practice it; if in workshops and factories there were danger to morals through the mixing of the sexes or from any occasion of evil; or if employers laid burdens upon the workmen which were unjust, or degraded them with conditions that were repugnant to their dignity as human beings; finally, if health were endangered by excessive labour, or by work unsuited to sex or age—in these cases there can be no question that within certain limits, it would be right to call in the help and authority of the law. The limits must be determined by the nature of the occasion which calls for the law's intervention—the principle being this, that *the law must not undertake more, nor go further, than is required for the remedy of the evil or the removal of the danger." Ibid.,* p. 188, #29.

PIUS XII: "In reality, besides commutative justice, there is also social justice with its own set obligations. . . . Now, it is of the very essence of social justice to demand from each individual all that is necessary for the common good. . . . It is impossible to care for the social organism and the good of society as a unit unless each single part and each individual member—that is to say, each individual man in the dignity of his human personality—is supplied with all that is necessary for the exercise of his social functions. . . . But social justice cannot be said to have been satisfied as long as working men are denied a salary that will enable them to secure proper sustenance for themselves and for their families; as long as they are denied the opportunity of acquiring a modest fortune . . . as long as they cannot make suitable provision through public or private insurance for old age, for periods of illness and unemployment. . . . It happens all too frequently, however, under the salary system, that individual employers are helpless to insure justice unless, with a view to its practice, they organize institutions the object of which is to prevent competition incompatible with fair treatment for the workers. Where this is true, it is the duty of contractors and employers to support and promote these institutions which are necessary to the fulfillment of the ends of justice." *Divini Redemptoris*, p. 362, #52; p. 363, #53 and 54.

LEO XIII: "If we turn now to things exterior and corporal, the first concern of all is to save the poor workers from the cruelty of grasping men who use human beings as mere instruments for making money. It is neither justice nor humanity so to grind men down with excessive labour as to stupefy their minds and wear out their bodies. . . . Daily labour, therefore, must be so regulated that it may not be protracted during longer hours than strength admits. How extended the intervals of rest should be will depend upon the nature of the work, on circumstances of time and place, and on the health and strength of the workman. . . . Then, again, the season of the year must be taken in account. . . . Finally, work which is suitable for a strong man cannot reasonably be required from a woman or a child. And, in regard to children, great care should be taken not to place them in workshops and factories until their bodies and minds are sufficiently mature. . . . Women, again, are not suited to certain trades. . . . As a general principle, it may be laid down, that a workman ought to have leisure and rest in proportion to the wear and tear of his strength. . . . In every contract between masters and work people, the condition is always express or understood that proper rest for soul and body be allowed. To agree in any other sense would be against what is right and just; for it can never be right or just to require on the one side, or to promise on the other, the giving up of those duties which a man owes to his God and to himself. . . ." *Rerum novarum*, pp. 191 and 192, #33.

"When workpeople take recourse to a strike, it is frequently because the hours of labour are too long, or the work too hard, or because they consider their wages insufficient. The grave inconvenience of this not uncommon occurrence should be obviated by public remedial measures; for such paralysis of labour not only affects the masters and their workpeople, but is extremely injurious to trade, and to the general interests of the public; moreover, on such occasions, violence and disorder are generally not far off, and thus it frequently happens that the public peace is threatened. The laws should be beforehand, and prevent these troubles from arising; they should lend their influence and authority to the removal in good time of the causes which lead to conflicts between masters and those whom they employ." *Rerum novarum,* pp. 189 and 190, #31.

130

Q. *Does the State alone have the capability of reorganizing economic life?*

A. Individual citizens, trade and labour unions, and welfare associations can contribute effectively to the reorganization of economic life. It is the duty of the State to respect and support their efforts, without absorbing or eliminating them, except when they should fail to procure the good of the individual or of the collectivity.

Leo XIII: "Finally, employers and workmen may themselves effect much in the matter of which We treat, by means of those institutions and organizations which afford opportune assistance to those in need, and which draw the two orders more closely together. Among these may be enumerated: societies for mutual help; various foundations established by private persons to provide for the workman and for his widow or his orphans, in sudden calamity, in sickness, and in the event of death; and what are called 'patronages,' or institutions for the care of boys and girls, for young people and also for those of more mature age. The most important of all are Workmen's Associations; for these virtually include all the rest. . . . Such associations should be adapted to the requirements of the age in which we live—an age of greater instruction, of different customs, and of more numerous requirements in daily life." *Rerum novarum*, p. 195, #36.

LEO XIII: "Let the State watch over these societies of citizens united together in the exercise of their right; but let it not thrust itself into their peculiar concerns and their organization. . . . In order that an association may be carried on with unity of purpose and harmony of action, its organization and government must be firm and wise. All such societies are not merely free to exist, but have the further right to adopt such rules and organizations as may best conduce to the attainment of their objects. We do not deem it possible to enter into definite details on the subject of organization; this must depend on national character, on practice and experience, on the nature and scope of the work to be done, on the magnitude of the various trades and employments, and on other circumstances of fact and of time—all of which must be carefully weighed. Speaking summarily, we may lay it down as a general and perpetual law, that workmen's associations should be so organized and governed as to furnish the best and most suitable means for attaining the end aimed at, that is to say, for helping each individual member to better his condition so far as he can, in body, mind, and property." *Rerum novarum*, p. 200, #41 and 42.

PIUS XI: "From this it is easy to conclude that in these associations the common interest of the whole 'Order' must predominate: and among these interests the most important is the directing of the activities of each trade [*artis*] to the common good. Regarding cases in which specific interests of employers and employees call for special care and protection, the parties, if such cases arise, will be able to deliberate separately, or come to a decision as the matter may require. . . . Here, too, men may choose whatever form they please, provided that both justice and the common good be taken into account." *Quadragesimo anno,* p. 210, #85 and 86.

131

Q. *Must the economy of a nation be run along democratic lines?*

A. The participation of the wage earners in the responsibility of directing the economic life of a nation would favour social cooperation, while a solidarity in the pursuit of the common good would improve the general conditions and the needs of the working man, enhancing his social improvement.

Pius XII: "The time has come to repudiate empty phrases, and to attempt to organize the forces of the people on a new basis; to raise them above the distinction between employers and would-be workers, and to realize that higher unity which is a bond between all those who cooperate in production, formed by their solidarity in the duty of working together for the common good and filling together the needs of the community. If this solidarity is extended to all branches of production, if it becomes the foundation for a better economic system, it will lead the working classes to obtain honestly their share of responsibility in the direction of the national economy. Thus, thanks to such harmonious coordination and cooperation, thanks to this closer unity of labor with the other elements of economic life, the worker will receive, as a result of his activity, a secure remuneration, sufficient to meet his needs and those of his family, together with spiritual satisfaction and a powerful incentive towards self-improvement." *Address to the Italian Catholic Workers' Association,* March 11, 1945.

Q. *Is international cooperation necessary for the reorganization of economic life?*

A. The reorganization of economic life must be effected by an easy exchange of services and goods even among nations in a spirit of collaboration and solidarity, striving to eliminate the burden of want that keeps many in a condition of pauperism, while some enjoy a monopolistically overabundant wealth.

PIUS XI: "In international trade relations let all means be sedulously employed for the removal of those artificial barriers to economic life which are the effects of distrust and hatred. All must remember that the peoples of the earth form but one family in God." *Divini Redemptoris.*

PIUS XII: "But also to nations as such we extend Our invitation to render operative this sense and obligation of solidarity: that every nation develop its potentialities in regard to living standards and employment, and contribute to a corresponding progress of nations less favored. Although even the most perfect realization of national solidarity would hardly bring about perfect equality among nations, still there is urgent need that this solidarity be put into practice, at least long enough to change perceptibly the present situation, which is far indeed from attaining a just harmony. In other words, solidarity among nations demands the abolition of glaring inequalities in living standards, and so in financial investments and in the degree of productivity of human labor." *Christmas Message,* 1952.

PIUS XII: "The natural riches of a region, a country, or a continent are destined not just for the economic profit of the few, but for the improvement of living conditions

—first of all material but also and paramountly moral and spiritual—of the groups of human beings who must live by exploitation of the earth's resources. The more and more apparent world character of economics and of the duties that fall upon privileged nations towards less favored ones will have their effect on the division of the goods produced." *Address to the World Petroleum Congress in Rome,* June 10, 1955.

Pius XII: "Peoples favored by nature or the progress of civilization are in danger of being rudely awakened one day, if they do not take the trouble henceforth to secure for the less fortunate the means to live in accordance with human dignity and to develop on their own account. To awaken further among a great number of individuals and nations this feeling of collective responsibility and above all to bring thereby enlightened and generous interventions about, is a lofty and noble task." *Address to Delegates of the United Nations Food and Agricultural Organization,* November 10, 1955.

133

Q. *Must a renewal of morals go together with the reform of institutions?*

A. A return to the gospel doctrine, the practice of religion, the notion that material goods are only means to an end, the exercise of justice and charity individually practiced are indispensable elements in the reorganizing of economic life.

Leo XIII: "But since religion alone, as We said at the beginning, can destroy the evil at its root, all men must be persuaded that the primary thing needful is to return to real Christianity, in the absence of which all the plans and devices of the wisest will be of little avail." *Rerum novarum* p. 204, #45.

Pius XI: "However, all that We have taught about reconstructing and perfecting the social order cannot be carried out without a reform of morals . . . a frank and sincere return to the teaching of the Gospel . . . all created goods as mere instruments under God, to be used only insofar as they help toward the attainment of our supreme end. . . . But, even though a state of things be pictured in which every man receives at last all that is his due, a wide field will nevertheless remain open for charity." *Quadragesimo anno*, p. 214, #97; p. 228, #136; p. 229, #137.

Pius XII: "One would say that humanity today, which has been able to build the marvellous and complex machine of the modern world, subjugating to its service the tremendous forces of nature, now appears incapable of controlling these forces, as though the rudder has slipped from its hands, and so it is in peril of being overthrown and crushed by them. Such inability to control should of itself suggest to men who are its victims not to expect salvation solely from technicians of production and organization. The work of these can help, and notably, to solve the grave and extensive problems which afflict the world, only if it is bound up with and directed toward bettering and strengthening true human values. But in no case will it avail to fashion a world without misery." *Christmas Message*, 1952.

Part Six

International Society

Chapter XIV. *The Human Community*

Chapter XV. *International Organization and Peace*

The Human Community

134

Q. *Is there a human society?*

A. In spite of the existence of individual independent
   States, the entire human kind constitutes one
   great society, with its own ends and laws.

Pius XII: "A disposition, in fact, of the divinely sanctioned natural order divides the human race into social
groups, nations or States, which are mutually independent in organization and in the direction of their
internal life. But for all that, the human race is bound
together by reciprocal ties, moral and juridical, into a
great commonwealth." *Summi Pontificatus,* p. 19, #72.

Pius XII: "The Catholic doctrine on the State and civil
society has always been based on the principle that, in
keeping with the will of God, the nations form together
a community with a common aim and common duties."
Christmas Message, 1948.

135

Q. *What is the end of human society?*

A. The end of human society is the common good
   of all peoples.

Pius XII: The human community is "directed to the
good of all nations. . . ." *Summi Pontificatus,* p. 19, #72.

Q. *Does human society have its laws by which it is governed?*

A. In the principles of international natural law, in the precepts of positive law and in lawful clauses contained in pacts concluded, human society has laws which protect its unity and promote its well-being.

Pius XII: "It is indispensable for the existence of harmonious and lasting contacts and of fruitful relations, that the peoples recognize and observe these principles of international natural law which regulate their normal development and activity. Such principles demand respect for corresponding rights to independence, to life and to the possibility of continuous development in the paths of civilization; they demand, further, fidelity to compacts agreed upon and sanctioned in conformity with the principles of the law of nations." *Summi Pontificatus,* p. 19, #74.

Pius XII: The international community is "ruled by special laws which protect its unity and promote prosperity." *Summi Pontificatus,* p. 19, #72.

Benedict XV: "The Gospel has not one law of charity for individuals and another for States and nations, which are indeed but collections of individuals." *Pacem, Dei munus pulcherrimum.*

Pius XI: "When, therefore, States and governments shall make it their sacred and solemn duty, in both domestic and foreign affairs, to follow the teaching and precepts of Christ, then they will enjoy the blessings of interior peace and of mutual confidence, and will find a peaceful settlement of any contentions that may arise." *Ubi arcano,* p. 17, #36.

Pius XII: "Such a new order, which all peoples desire to see brought into being after the trials and the ruins of this war, must be founded on that immovable and unshakable rock, the moral law which He has engraved with indelible characters in the hearts of men: that moral law whose observance must be inculcated and fostered by the public opinion of all nations and of all States with such a unanimity of voice and energy that no one may dare to call into doubt or weaken its binding force." *Christmas Message,* 1941.

137

Q. *Is the unity of human society broken by the evolution, the differentiation and the organization of individual peoples into States?*

A. The evolution, differentiation, and organization of the various peoples into States do not break but rather enrich the human family if the exchange of benefits obtained through such processes is effected peacefully.

Pius XII: "And the nations, despite a difference of development due to diverse conditions of life and of culture, are not destined to break the unity of the human race, but rather to enrich and embellish it by the sharing of their own peculiar gifts and by that reciprocal interchange of goods which can be possible and efficacious only when a mutual love and a lively sense of charity unite all the sons of the same Father and all those redeemed by the same Divine Blood." *Summi Pontificatus,* p. 12, #43.

138

Q. *Does Christian doctrine strengthen the community of mankind?*

A. Christian doctrine teaches the brotherhood of man, which embraces love for country, according to rational order in man's affections.

Pius XII: "Nor is there any fear lest the consciousness of universal brotherhood aroused by the teaching of Christianity, and the spirit which it inspires, be in contrast with love of traditions or the glories of one's fatherland, or impede the progress of prosperity or legitimate interests. For that same Christianity teaches that in the exercise of charity we must follow a God-given order, yielding the place of honour in our affections and good works to those who are bound to us by special ties. . . . But legitimate and well-ordered love of our native country should not make us close our eyes to the all-embracing nature of Christian charity, which calls for consideration of others and their interests in the pacifying light of love." *Summi Pontificatus*, p. 14, #49.

139

Q. *Does love of country exclude love of mankind?*

A. A love of country which does not exclude love of mankind leads to many virtuous deeds, but it can become the cause of grave dangers and damage for the human community if vitiated by a blind nationalism.

Pius XI: "For love of country and of race, though a spur to many deeds of virtue and heroism when guided by Christianity, may become also the seed of widespread injustice and iniquity when it transgresses the bounds of right and justice, developing into a spirit of excessive nationalism. They who fall into this error surely forget that all peoples, as members of the universal human family, are linked together by the common ties of brotherhood; that other nations also have a right to live and to seek prosperity; and that it is neither permissible nor expedient to divorce the pursuit of the useful from the practice of honesty. For 'justice exalteth a nation, but sin maketh nations miserable' (Prov. 14:34). That a family, a city, or a State should have acquired advantages at the expense of its neighbours may seem to some a brilliant and splendid achievement, still Augustine wisely warns us that such achievements are neither lasting nor exempt from fear of disaster. . . ." *Ubi arcano*, p. 12, #20.

Pius XII: "But the real error consists in confusing national life in its proper sense with nationalistic politics: the first, the right and prized possession of a people, may and should be promoted; the second, as a form infinitely harmful, will never be sufficiently repelled." *Christmas Message*, 1954.

International Organization and Peace

***

140

Q. *What are the principal dangers militating against a sound human society?*

A. The principle of the accomplished fact or that of force, the conception of a State possessing unlimited power, internal disorder, injustice and nationalistic egotism are the main dangers militating against a sound human society.

PIUS IX: "There are those who say that in the political order, the accomplished fact, by the very fact that it is accomplished, has the force of law." *Quanta cura.*

LEO XIII: "The iniquitous principle that has consecrated the law of force as the supreme law of the world. . . ." *Giunti al venticinquesimo anno.*

PIUS XII: "The idea which credits the States with unlimited authority is not simply an error harmful to the internal life of nations, to their prosperity, and to the larger and well-ordered increase in their well-being, but likewise it injures the relations between peoples, for it breaks the unity of supra-national society, robs the law of nations of its foundation and vigour, leads to violation of others' rights and impedes agreement and peaceful intercourse." *Summi Pontificatus*, p. 18, #71.

PIUS XI: "And from these unrestrained lusts, masquerading under the guise of the public weal and patriotism, have often sprung enmity and conflicts among nations. For love of country and of race, though a spur to many deeds of virtue and heroism when guided by Christianity, may become also the seed of widespread injustice and iniquity when it transgresses the bounds of right and justice, developing into a spirit of excessive nationalism." *Ubi arcano*, p. 12, #20.

Pius XII: "International relations and internal order are intimately related. International equilibrium and harmony depend on the internal equilibrium and development of the individual States in the material, social and intellectual spheres. A firm and steady peace policy toward other nations is, in fact, impossible without a spirit of peace within the nation which inspires trust. It is only then, by striving for an integral peace, a peace in both fields, that peoples will be freed from the cruel nightmare of war, and the material and psychological causes of further discord and disorder will be diminished." *Christmas Message*, 1942.

141

Q. *Is "Cold War" a dangerous condition?*

A. Fear is the underlying factor in the present international situation in which one sees the opposing groups tolerate each other so as not to perish, limiting themselves to coexistence rather than existence in peaceful relations. This method eliminates none of the dangers deeply rooted in the situation.

Pius XII: "It is a common impression, derived from the simple observation of facts, that the principal foundation on which the present state of relative calm rests is fear. Each of the groups into which the human family is divided tolerates the existence of the other, because it does not wish itself to perish. But thus avoiding a fatal risk, the two groups do not live together: they coexist. It is not a state of war, but neither is it peace; it is a cold calm. . . . The most obvious absurdity of the situation resultant from such a wretched state of affairs is this: current political practice, while dreading war as the greatest of catastrophes, at the same time puts all its trust in war, as if it were the only expedient for subsistence and the only means of regulating international relations. This is, in a certain sense, placing trust in that which is loathed above all other things." *Christmas Message,* 1954.

Pius XII: "It is clear that simple coexistence does not deserve the name of peace, to which Christian tradition, formed in the school of the lofty intellects of Augustine and Thomas Aquinas, has come to apply the definition 'the tranquillity of order.' Cold peace is only a provisional calm whose duration is conditioned upon the changeable sensation of fear and upon the varying calculation of present strength: while it has about it nothing of 'true order,' which presupposes a series of relationships converging towards a common purpose that is right and just. Besides, by excluding all bonds of a spiritual nature between peoples so fragmentarily coexisting, cold peace falls far short of that which was preached and desired by the Divine Master: for His peace is founded on a union of souls in the same truth and in charity. It is defined by St. Paul as the 'peace of God' which binds in the first place men's minds and hearts (Phil. 4:7), and it is put into practice by acts of harmonious collaboration in every field of life, not excluding the political, social and economic fields." *Christmas Message,* 1954.

Pius XII: "The present coexistence in fear has thus only two possible prospects before it: either it will raise itself to a coexistence in fear of God, and thence to a truly peaceful living-together, inspired and protected by the divine moral order; or else it will shrivel more and more into a frozen paralysis of international life, the grave dangers of which are even now foreseeable." *Christmas Message,* 1954.

PIUS XII: "There is, in fact, some hope that today's coexistence may bring mankind closer to peace. In order, however, that this expectation be justified, such coexistence must in some way be coexistence in truth. Now, a bridge cannot be built in truth between these two separate worlds unless it be founded on the human beings living in one and the other of these worlds, and not on their governmental or social systems." *Christmas Message,* 1954.

PIUS XII: "Efforts toward peace must consist not only in measures aimed at restricting the possibility of waging war, but even more in preventing, eliminating or lessening with time the quarrels between nations which might lead to war." *Christmas Message,* 1954.

142

Q. *What are the essential prerequisites for a lasting peace?*

A. The essential prerequisites for a lasting peace are the following: 1) respect for the life and independence of every nation; 2) renunciation of the principle of recourse to force; 3) international juridical reorganization; 4) recognition of the real needs of nations and of minorities; 5) use of the sense of responsibility enlightened by divine law.

PIUS XII: "The fundamental conditions of a just and honourable peace are: 1) to assure the right to life and independence of all nations, large and small, strong or weak. . . . 2) Nations must be liberated from the heavy slavery of armaments and the danger that material force, instead of serving to protect rights, become the tyrannical violator of them. . . . 3) Any reorganization of internal neighbourliness should conform with the maximum of human wisdom for all parties concerned. . . . And in creating or reconstructing international institutions which have a mission so high but at the same time difficult and full of serious responsibilities, account should be taken of experiences which arose from the efficacy or defective functioning of similar previous projects . . . realizing that the establishment of juridical institutions which would serve to guarantee the loyal and faithful carrying out of terms and, in case of recognized need, the revising and correcting of them, is of decisive importance. . . . 4) A point which should be given particular attention . . . concerns the real needs and just demands of nations and peoples as well as of ethnic minorities. . . . 5) Those who guide the destinies of peoples, and the peoples themselves, must not refuse to permit themselves to be penetrated by a spirit . . . of intimate, acute responsibility that measures and weighs human statutes according to the holy, unshakable rules of Divine Law." *Christmas Message,* 1939.

Pius XII: "The first postulate of every action towards peace is the recognition of the existence of a natural law, common to all men and to all nations, from which flow the guiding principles of existence, of action and of obligation, and the observance of which facilitates and guarantees men's living and working side by side for mutual advantage." *Address to Members of the Italian Study Center for International Reconciliation,* Oct. 13, 1955.

143

Q. *What are the conditions for the restoration of a new international order?*

A. In order to attain a restoration of international society (an indispensable prerequisite for a lasting peace), it is necessary, 1) to eliminate motives derived from hatred; 2) to respect pacts; 3) to avoid judging as just what is useful; 4) to reorder economic life by eliminating injustice and poverty; 5) to practice sincere juridical and economic solidarity among the States.

Pius XII: "The necessary premises for such a new order are as follows: 1) Victory over the hatred which divides the nations today and the disappearance of systems and actions which breed this hatred. 2) Victory over distrust, which exerts a paralyzing pressure on international law and makes all honest understanding impossible. Return to the loyalty treaties without which the secure cooperation of nations and especially the living side by side of strong and weak nations are inconceivable. 3) Victory over the dismal principle that utility is the foundation and aim of law, and that might can create right. This principle is bound to upset all international relations and is inacceptable to all weaker nations. This conception does not exclude the desire for the honourable improvement of conditions or the right to defend oneself if peaceful life has been attacked, or to repair the damage sustained hereby. 4) Victory over those potential conflicts arising out of the disequilibrium of world economy. Therefore, a new economic order is to be gradually evolved which gives all nations the means to secure for their citizens an appropriate standard of life. 5) Victory over the kind of egoism which, relying on its own power, aims at impairing the honour and liberty of individuals. This egoism has to be replaced by a genuine Christian solidarity of a legal and economic character, and by a brotherly cooperation of the nations, the sovereignty of which has been duly secured." *Christmas Message*, 1940.

Pius XII: "There remains no other way to salvation than that of repudiating definitely the idolatry of absolute nationalism, the pride of race and blood, the desire for hegemony in the possession of worldly goods, and to turn resolutely toward the spirit of sincere fraternity which is founded on the worship of the Divine Father of all men." *Address to the People of Rome*, March 18, 1945.

144

Q. *What must be the aim of a new international order?*

A. A new international order must seek 1) the respect of every nation; 2) the respect of minorities; 3) international economic collaboration; 4) progressive disarmament, arbitration, revision of treaties; 5) respect of religion.

Pius XII: "Within the limits of a new order founded on moral principles, 1) there is no room for the violation of the freedom, integrity and security of other States, no matter what may be their territorial extension or their capacity for defense. . . . 2) There is no place for open or occult oppression of the cultural and linguistic characteristics of national minorities, for the hindrance or restriction of their economic resources, for the limitation or abolition of their natural fertility. . . . 3) There is no place for that cold and calculating egotism which tends to hoard the economic resources and materials destined for the use of all to such an extent that the nations less favored by nature are not permitted access to them. . . . 4) Once the more dangerous sources of armed conflicts have been eliminated, there is no place for a total warfare or for a mad rush to armaments. . . . It is essential to proceed with sincerity and honesty to a progressive limitation of armaments. . . . Certain institutions must be established which will merit the respect of all and which will dedicate themselves to the most noble office of guaranteeing the sincere observance of treaties, and of promoting, in accordance with the principles of law and equity, necessary corrections and revisions of such treaties. . . . 5) There is no place for the persecution of religion and of the Church." *Christmas Message,* 1941.

145

Q. *Is the constitution of an association of nations a desirable thing?*

A. A permanent association of nations is useful in order to guarantee the independence of the States and international order.

BENEDICT XV: "It is much to be desired . . . that all States, putting aside mutual suspicion, should unite in one league, or rather a sort of family of peoples, calculated both to maintain their own independence and safeguard the order of human society. What specially, amongst other reasons, calls for such an association of nations, is the need generally recognized of making every effort to abolish or reduce the enormous burden of the military expenditures which States can no longer bear, in order to prevent these disastrous wars or at least to remove the danger of them as far as possible. So would each nation be assured not only of its independence but also of the integrity of its territory within its just frontiers." *Pacem, Dei munus pulcherrimum.*

PIUS XII: "An essential point in any future international arrangement would be the formation of an organ for the maintenance of peace, of an organ invested by common consent with supreme power, to whose office it would also pertain to smother in its germinal state any threat of isolated or collective aggression. But on one condition: that the peace settlement, which should be strengthened and made more stable by mutual guarantees and, where necessary, by economic sanctions and even armed intervention, should provide vigour and stability, and should definitely not give countenance to any injustice, nor allow the infringement of any right to the detriment of any people, nor continue any imposition or tribute, which latter can be permitted only temporarily as reparations for war damages." *Christmas Message,* 1944.

146

Q. *Does a society of nations require a common authority?*

A. It is necessary that an international society be organized according to democratic lines, but with an effective authority to which all member States shall give due obedience.

Pius XII: "One understands why the authority of such a society must be real and effective over the member States, in such wise, however, that each of them retain an equal right of its own sovereignty. Only thus will the spirit of sane democracy be able to pervade that vast and thorny ground of foreign relations." *Christmas Message,* 1944.

147

Q. *Is European unity desirable?*

A. A multiplicity of reasons make European unity greatly desirable, since with it are connected obvious economic and social benefits for its peoples and the peaceful safeguard of their common civilization.

Pius XII: "This can and should be done in Europe, by

forming the continental union of its peoples, different indeed, but geographically and historically bound together. A strong encouragement to such a union is the manifest failure of the contrary policy, and the fact that the ordinary people in these countries expect it and consider it necessary and possible. The time, then, seems mature for the idea to become reality." *Christmas Message*, 1953.

Pius XII: "The efforts being made at present to give unity to Europe—whatever the method of unification might be, provided it proves effective—also entail the setting up of new conditions for its economic development. . . . Without doubt, the advantages of a European economy do not consist simply in the unified and extended area in which the so-called mechanism of the market would regulate production and consumption. It is even more important, within the limits of competition, to aim not only at the construction of a European economy but also at a stabilization of a truly social life, and at a healthy development of the family from one generation to another; and under this aspect and with this end in view, the natural criteria should be made to prevail regarding the organization of production in space and time, and a rational consumption." *Address to Italian Workers*, May 1, 1953.

Pius XII: "During this last decade since the war, a great yearning for spiritual renovation urges souls to unite Europe strongly, the impetus coming from the natural living conditions of her peoples, with the purpose of putting an end to traditional rivalries between one another, and of assuring a united protection for their independence and their peaceful development. . . . The succeeding events no longer have for a basis the ideal of a more extensive European unification. . . . Europe, on the other hand, still awaits the reawakening of her own consciousness. . . . In any case, that which must remain, and without doubt will remain, is the genuine Europe, that is, that composite of all the spiritual and civil values which the West has accumulated, drawing from the riches of individual nations to dispense them to the whole world. Europe, conforming to the dispositions of Divine Providence, will again be able to be the nursery and dispenser of those values, if she will know how to resume wisely her proper spiritual character and to repudiate the divinization of power." *Christmas Message*, 1954.

148

Q. *Is a war of aggression a suitable means of solving international controversies?*

A. A war of aggression is neither a lawful nor a necessary means of solving international controversies nor the proper means toward realizing national aspirations.

Pius XII: "There is a duty, besides, imposed on all, a duty which brooks no delay, no procrastination, no hesitation, no subterfuge: it is the duty to do everything to ban once and for all wars of aggression as a legitimate solution of international disputes and as a means toward realizing national aspirations." *Christmas Message*, 1944.

Pius XII: "The absurdity [is evident] of that doctrine which held . . . that war is one of many admissible forms of political action, the necessary, and as it were the natural, outcome of irreconcilable disputes between two countries; and that war, therefore, is a fact bearing no relation to any kind of moral responsibility. It is likewise apparent how absurd and inadmissible is the principle . . . according to which a ruler who declares war would only be guilty of having made a political error should the war be lost. But he could in no case be accused of moral guilt and of crime for not having preserved peace, when he was able to do so." *Christmas Message*, 1954.

PIUS XII: "An unnecessary war [is an] awful crime." *Christmas Message*, 1954.

PIUS XII: "Unjust war is to be accounted as one of the gravest crimes which international penal law must proscribe, must punish with the heaviest penalties. . . . Even in a just war, attempts to victory are not all defensible in the eyes of those who have an exact and reasonable concept of justice." *Address to Members of the Congress of International Penal Law*, October 3, 1953.

Index

Abortion, 50–51; Pius XI on, 50–51
Administrators, public, special duties of, 90–91
Adultery, Pius XI on, 50
Aggression, war of, 195–96; Pius XII on, 195–96
Association, man's right of, 10–11; Leo XIII on, 10
Atheism, 75
Authoritarianism, 77; Pius XII on, 77
Authority
  disobedience to permitted, Leo XIII on, 35–36
  doctrine of divine origin of
    benefits of, 31–32; Leo XIII on, 31–32
    denial of, 28–29; Leo XIII on, 28–29
    social dangers of, 29–31; Leo XIII on, 30–31
  errors concerning origin of, 26–28; Leo XIII on, 27–28
  insurrection against, 36–37; Leo XIII on, 36–37; Pius XI on, 37
  obedience due, 35; Leo XIII on, 35
  proper exercise of, 33; Leo XIII on, 33
  purpose of, 32–33; Leo XIII on, 33
  respect due, 35; Leo XIII on, 35
  society's, 25–26; Leo XIII on, 25; Pius XII on, 25–26
  source of, 26; Leo XIII on, 26; Pius XII on, 26

Beatific Vision, the, 4
Benedict XV, Pope
  on association of nations, 192
  on human society, 180
Business, socialization of, 164–65; Pius XII on, 165

Capital, conflict of with labour, 147–48; Leo XIII on, 147; Pius XI on, 147
Catholics
  and the evil of abstention from public life, 85–86; Leo XIII on, 85; Pius X on, 86
  and participation in public life, 82–86
  and political parties, 89–90; Pius XI on, 89; Leo XIII on, 89; Pius X on, 90
Christian doctrine and brotherhood, 181–82; Pius XII on, 182

Church, the
  concerns of, 97; Pius XI on, 97; Pius XII on, 97; Leo XIII on,
    97
  definition of, 95–96; Leo XIII on, 95–96; Pius XII on, 96
  and discipline concerning matrimony, 47; Leo XIII on, 47
  as distinct form of society, 22–23; Pius XI on, 23
  duties of State toward, 108
  and economic life, 134–35, 136
  end of, 96; Leo XIII on, 96
  and government, 103; Leo XIII on, 103
  jurisdiction of, 109; Leo XIII on, 109
  and political questions, 101–02; Leo XIII on, 102; Pius XI on,
    102; Pius XII on, 101–02
  rights of, 98–99; Leo XIII on, 98–99; Pius X on, 98; Pius XI
    on, 99
  and socio-economic questions, 99–101; Leo XIII on, 99; Pius
    XI on, 99–101; Pius XII on, 101
  and State laws, 108–09; Leo XIII on, 108–09
  supremacy of, 96–97, 105–06; Leo XIII on, 96–97, 105–06
Church-State collaboration, 106–08, 111–12; Leo XIII on, 106–
  07, 112; Pius XI on, 107–08
Church-State relations, errors regarding, 112–15; Leo XIII on,
  112–15
Citizens
  directives governing public activities of, 86–87; Pius XII on,
    86–87
  obligation of to public life, 81–82; Leo XIII on, 81; Pius XI
    on, 81; Pius XII on, 81–82
Citizens, Catholic
  obligation to public life, 82–85; Leo XIII on, 83, 84–85; Pius
    X on, 82–83; Pius XI on, 83
Cold War, the, 186–88; Pius XII on, 186–88
Communism, Pius XI on, 76, 126–30; Pius XII on, 130
Concordats, definition of, 112; Leo XIII on, 112
Cooperation, international,
  and economic life, 174–75

Democracy, Leo XIII on, 73; Pius XII on, 73
  conditions necessary for, 74–75; Pius XII on, 74–75
  and economic life, 173; Pius XII on, 173
Divorce, Pius XI on, 52
  evil effects of, 53–54; Leo XIII on, 53–54

Economic activity, purpose of, 153–54; Pius XI on, 153–54;
  Pius XII on, 154

Economic disorder, factors producing, 121–23; Leo XIII on, 121–22; Pius XII on, 122–23

Economic life
and the Church, 134–35, 136; Leo XIII on, 134–35, 136; Pius XI on, 136; Pius XII on, 135
democracy in, 173
rationalization of, 154–56, 157; Pius XI on, 155, 157; Pius XII on, 155–56
reorganization of, 133–34; Pius XI on, 133; Pius XII on, 133–34
international cooperation in, 174–75
and morals, 175–76
and State, 159–60, 171–73
and technical progress, 157–58; Pius XII on, 157–58

Economic order
and diversity of men, 137–38; Leo XIII on, 137–38; Pius XII on, 138
and individual rights, 119–21; Leo XIII on, 121; Pius XI on, 119–21; Pius XII on, 121
and materialism, 126–30; Pius XI on, 126–30; Pius XII on, 130

Economic welfare, State and, 70–77
Education, State obligations toward, 65–66
Employees, duties of to employers, 148–50; Leo XIII on, 149–50
Employers, duties of to employees, 148–50
Eugenics, Pius XI on, 50–51

Family
Catholic constitution of, 42–43; Leo XIII on, 43
definition of, 41–42; Leo XIII on, 41; Pius XI on, 42
eternal laws governing, 42; Pius XI on, 42
guarantees for well-being of, 55–56; Leo XIII on, 55–56; Pius XI on, 56
integration of in State, 56–58; Leo XIII on, 56–57; Pius XI on, 57–58

Free competition, 125–26; Pius XI on, 125; Pius XII on, 125–26
Free will, man's, 3; Leo XIII on, 3

God, society's duty toward, 16; Leo XIII on, 16; Pius XII on, 16
Government
forms of, 72–73; Leo XIII on, 73; Pius XII on, 73
unsuitable forms of, 75–77; Pius XI on, 76–77; Pius XII on, 77

Hereditary transmission, right of, 141; Leo XIII on, 141

Human society

dangers against, 185–86; Leo XIII on, 185; Pius IX on, 185;
Pius XI on, 185–86; Pius XII on, 185, 186
definition of, 179; Pius XII on, 179
end of, 179; Pius XII on, 179
laws regarding, 180–81; Benedict XV on, 180; Pius XI on, 180;
Pius XII on, 180, 181
unity of, 181; Pius XII on, 181

Indissolubility, as property of matrimony, 45–46
Institutions, reforming of, 158–59, 162; Pius XI on, 159
Intelligence, man's, 3
International society
aim of, 191–92; Pius XII on, 191–92
prerequisites for, 189–91; Pius XII on, 190–91

Jurisdiction, mixed, 109–10; Leo XIII on, 110
and education of youth, 110–11; Pius XI on, 110–11
and harmony, 111; Leo XIII on, 111
and matrimony, 110–11; Leo XIII on, 110

Labour
conflict of with capital, 147–48; Leo XIII on, 147; Pius XI on,
147–48
end of, 140–41; Leo XIII on, 140–41
purpose of organized, 150–51; Pius XII on, 150–51
Laws, human, foundation of, 33–34; Leo XIII on, 34
Leo XIII, Pope
on attitude toward riches, 146
on authority of society, 25
on benefits of doctrine of divine origin of authority, 31–32
on Catholic constitution of family, 43
on Catholic obligation to public life, 83, 84–85
on Catholics and political parties, 89
on Church, 95–96
on Church and economic life, 134–35
on Church and government, 103
on Church and laws of State, 108–09
on Church and matrimony, 47
on Church and political parties, 88–89
on Church and political questions, 102
on Church and socio-economic questions, 99
on Church-State supremacy, 105–06
on citizen obligation to public life, 81

on civil effects of matrimony, 48
on civil society, 20
on concerns of Church, 97
on concordats, 112
on dangers to human society, 185
on definition of family, 41
on definition of State, 61
on denial of divine origin of authority, 28–29
on disobedience to authority, 35–36
on diversity of men, 137–38
on divine origin of society, 15–16
on economic disorder, 121–22
on employee and employer duties, 149–50
on end of Church, 96
on end of labour, 140–41
on end of society, 18
on ends of matrimony, 44
on errors concerning authority, 27–28
on errors regarding Church-State relations, 112–15
on evil effects of divorce, 53–54
on evil of Catholic abstention from public life, 85
on exercise of man's rights, 12–13
on family-State integration, 56–57
on forms of government, 73
on foundation of human laws, 34
on fruition of man's rights, 13
on guarantees for family well-being, 55–56
on hereditary transmission, 141
on inalienability of man's rights, 11
on indissolubility of marriage, 53
on individual economic rights, 121
on insurrection against authority, 36–37
on jurisdiction of Church and State, 109
on just wage, 152
on labour-capital conflict, 147
on limitations of State, 63–64
on man's free will, 3
on man's right to achieve ultimate end, 7
on man's superior dignity, 4, 5
on matrimonial jurisdiction, 110
on mixed jurisdiction, 110
on moral reform, 175
on non-sacramental matrimony, 45
on obedience due authority, 35
on order of society, 21–22

on origin of society, 15
on political parties, 87
on private ownership, 138–39, 140
on private society, 19–20
on proper exercise of authority, 33
on properties of matrimony, 46
on purpose of authority, 33
on regulation of private ownership, 142
on religious duties of State, 67–69
on respect due authority, 35
on right of association, 10
on right to propagate, 8
on right of State to regulate private ownership, 162–63
on right to worldly goods, 9
on rights of Church, 98–99
on separation of consorts, 53
on social danger of denial of authority's divine origin, 30–31
on social function of ownership, 144
on society's duty to God, 16
on source of authority, 26
on State and economic life, 171–72
on State and economic welfare, 71
on State exercise of power, 78
on State as protector of liberty, 69–70
on State and public prosperity, 72
on supremacy of Church, 96–97
on types of society, 19
on working class, 167–69, 170–71
Liberalism, Leo XIII on, 27–28, 29
Liberty, State as protector of, 69–70
Life, man's right to, 6–7; Pius XI on, 6; Pius XII on, 6–7
Love of country, Pius XI on, 182–83; Pius XII on, 183

Man
    body of, 3
    nature of, 3
    origin of, 3
    right of to achieve ultimate end, 7; Leo XIII on, 7; Pius X on,
        7; Pius XI on, 7
    rights of, 5–6; Pius XI on, 5; Pius XII on, 5–6
    soul of, 3; Pius XI on, 3
    superior dignity of, 4–5; Leo XIII on, 4, 5; Pius XI on, 4, 5
    ultimate end of, 4; Pius XI on, 4
Marriage, Christian, Leo XIII on, 43
    indissolubility of, 53; Leo XIII on, 53

modern fallacies regarding, 48–52; Pius XI on, 48–52
Matrimony
  benefits from indissolubility of, 54–55; Pius XI on, 54–55
  civil effects of, 47–48; Leo XIII on, 48
  discipline concerning, 47
  ends of, 43–45; Leo XIII on, 44; Pius XI on, 43–45
  and mixed jurisdiction, 110
  non-sacramental, 45; Leo XIII on, 45
  properties of, 45–46; Leo XIII on, 46; Pius XI on, 45–46
Microcosm, man as, 4
Monopoly and economic disorder, 125–26
Morals, and economic reform, 175–76

Nations
  association of, 192–93; Benedict XV on, 192; Pius XII on, 192–93
  authority for, 193; Pius XII on, 193
Naturalism, Leo XIII on, 27–28

Officials, elected, special duties of, 90–91; Pius X on, 90; Pius XI on, 91; Pius XII on, 90–91
Ownership
  community, 164; Pius XI on, 164
  private
    regulation of, 141–43; Leo XIII on, 142; Pius XII on, 142–43
    right to, 138–40; Leo XIII, 138–39, 140; Pius XI on, 139; Pius XII on, 139, 140
    right of State to regulate, 162–63; Leo XIII on, 162–63; Pius XI on, 163; Pius XII on, 163
    social function of, 143–44; Pius XI on, 143–44; Leo XIII on, 144
    and use of property, 144–45; Pius XI on, 145; Pius XII on, 145

Peace, prerequisites for, 188–89; Pius XII on, 188–89
Pius IX, Pope
  on dangers to human society, 185
  on practice of religion, 17
Pius X, Pope
  on Catholic obligation to public life, 82–83
  on Catholics and political parties, 90
  on duties of public officials, 90
  on evil of Catholic abstention from public life, 86
  on man's right to achieve ultimate end, 7
  on rights of Church, 98

Pius XI, Pope

on abortion, 50–51
on adultery, 50
on attitude toward riches, 146–147
on benefits from indissolubility of marriage, 54–55
on Catholic obligation to public life, 83
on Catholics and political parties, 89
on Church as distinct form of society, 22–23
on Church and political questions, 102
on Church and socio-economic questions, 99–101
on citizen's obligation to public life, 81
on civil society, 23
on common good to be attained by State, 63
on Communism, 76, 126–30
on community ownership, 164
on concerns of Church, 97
on dangers to human society, 185–86
on definition of family, 42
on definition of State, 61
on distribution of wealth, 165–66
on divorce, 52
on duties of public officials, 91
on economic activity, 153–54
on economic life, 155, 157
on educational jurisdiction, 110–11
on educational mission of State, 65–66
on end of society, 17
on end of State, 62
on ends of matrimony, 43–45
on eternal laws governing family, 42
on eugenics, 50–51
on family-State integration, 57–58
on free competition, 125
on fruition of man's rights, 13
on guarantees for family well-being, 56
on human society, 180
on inalienability of man's rights, 11
on individual economic rights, 119–21
on insurrection against authority, 37
on international cooperation, 174–75
on just wage, 153
on labour-capital conflict, 147–48
on love of country, 182–83
on man's duty to remain in society, 18
on man's rights, 5

on man's right to achieve ultimate end, 7
on man's soul, 3
on man's superior dignity, 4, 5
on man's ultimate end, 4
on modern fallacies regarding marriage, 48–52
on moral reform, 176
on necessary societies, 21
on perfecting of society, 19
on perfect society, 20
on political parties, 87–88
on private ownership, 139
on properties of matrimony, 45–46
on reforming of institutions, 159
on religious duties of State, 68
on reorganization of economic life, 133
on right to life, 6
on right to propagate, 8
on right of State to regulate private ownership, 163
on right to worldly goods, 9
on rights of Church, 99
on sanctifying grace, 3
on social function of ownership, 143–44
on Socialism, 76–77
on State and economic life, 172–73
on State and economic welfare, 71
on State intervention, 161
on totalitarianism, 76
on unsuitable forms of government, 76–77
on use of property, 145
Pius XII, Pope
on aim of international society, 191–92
on association of nations, 192–93
on authoritarianism, 77
on authority of society, 25–26
on Church, 96
on Church and economic life, 135
on Church and political questions, 101–02
on Church and socio-economic questions, 101
on citizen obligation to public life, 81–82
on Cold War, 186–88
on Communism, 130
on concerns of Church, 97
on conditions necessary for democracy, 74–75
on dangers to human society, 185, 186
and definition of State, 61

on democracy in economic life, 173
on directives governing citizen's public activities, 86–87
on distribution of wealth, 166–67
on diversity of men, 138
on duties of public officials, 90–91
on economic activity, 154
on economic disorder, 122–23
on economic life, 155–56
on end of society, 18
on end of State, 62
on European unity, 193–95
on forms of government, 73
on free competition, 125–26
on human society, 179
on inalienability of man's rights, 12
on individual economic rights, 121
on just peace, 188–89
on laws governing human society, 180, 181
on limitations of state, 63, 64–65
on love of country, 183
on man's rights, 5–6
on moral reform, 176
on prerequisites for international society, 190–91
on private ownership, 139, 140, 163
on purpose of organized labour, 150–51
on regulation of private ownership, 142–43
on reorganization of economic life, 133–34
on right to life, 6–7
on right to worldly goods, 9
on socialization of business, 165
on social order, 131
on society's duty to God, 16
on source of authority, 26
on State exercise of power, 78–80
on State intervention, 161
on technical progress, 157–58
on totalitarianism, 77
on unity of human society, 181
on unjust war, 195–96
on unsuitable forms of government, 77
on use of property, 145
on working class, 169–70
Political parties
Church position regarding, 88–89; Leo XIII on, 88–89
legality of existence of, 87–88; Leo XIII on, 87; Pius XI on, 87–88

Power
  State and exercise of, 78–80
Propagation, man's right of, 8; Leo XIII on, 8; Pius XI on, 8
Public life
  Catholic participation in, 82–86
  citizen obligation concerning, 81–82
Public prosperity, State and, 72

Rationalism, Leo XIII on, 27, 29
Religion, practice of, 17; Pius IX on, 17
Riches, man's attitude toward, 146–47; Leo XIII on, 146; Pius
    XI on, 146–47
Rights of man
  exercise of, 12–13; Leo XIII on, 12–13
  fruition of, 13; Leo XIII on, 13; Pius XI on, 13
  inalienability of, 11–12; Leo XIII on, 11; Pius XI on, 11; Pius
    XII on, 12

St. Augustine, on marriage, 46
St. Thomas, on private society, 20
Sanctifying grace, effect of, 3; Pius XI on, 3
Separation of consorts, 52–53; Leo XIII on, 53
Socialism, Pius XI on, 76–77, 129–30
Social order and moral reform, 130–31; Pius XII on, 131
Society
  civil, 19–20; Leo XIII on, 20; definition of, 61; Leo XIII on,
    61; Pius XI on, 61; Pius XII on, 61
  conventional, 20
  divine origin of, 15–16; Leo XIII on, 15–16
  duty of toward God, 16; Leo XIII on, 16; Pius XII on, 16
  end of, 17–18; Leo XIII on, 18; Pius XI on, 17; Pius XII on,
    18
  imperfect, 20
  man's duty to remain in, 18; Pius XI on, 18
  natural, 20–21; Pius XI on, 21; pre-eminent type of, 23; Pius
    XI on, 23
  order of, 21–22; Leo XIII on, 21–22
  origin of, 15; Leo XIII on, 15
  perfect, 20; Pius XI on, 20
  perfecting of, 18–19; Pius XI on, 19
  private, 19–20; Leo XIII on, 20
  public, 20
  supernatural, 20–21; Pius XI on, 21
  types of, 19; Leo XIII on, 19
Soul, man's, Leo XIII on, 4
State
  and civil effects of matrimony, 47–48; Leo XIII on, 48

common good to be attained by, 62–63; Pius XI on, 63

definition of, 61; Leo XIII on, 61; Pius XI on, 61; Pius XIII on, 61

duties of to Church, 108; Leo XIII on, 108; Pius XI on, 108

and economic welfare, 70–71; Leo XIII on, 71; Pius XI on, 71

educational mission of, 65–66; Pius XI on, 65–66

end of, 61–62; Pius XI on, 62; Pius XII on, 62

exercise of power of, 78–80; Leo XIII on, 78; Pius XII on, 78–80

guarantees against arbitrary exercise of power of, 78–80

integration of family in, 56–58; Leo XIII on, 56–57; Pius XI on, 57–58

jurisdiction of, 109

limitations of, 63–65; Leo XIII on, 63–64; Pius XII on, 63, 64–65

as pre-eminent natural society, 23

as protector of liberty, 69–70; Leo XIII on, 69–70

and public prosperity, 72; Leo XIII on, 72

and regulation of production, 160–61; Pius XI on, 161; Pius XII on, 161

religious duties of, 67–69; Leo XIII on, 67–69; Pius XI on, 68

and reorganization of economic life, 159–60; Leo XIII on, 160; Pius XI on, 160

right of to regulate private ownership, 162–63; Leo XIII on, 162–63; Pius XI on, 163; Pius XII on, 163

supremacy of, 105–06; Leo XIII on, 105–06

and wealth distribution, 165–67; Pius XI on, 165–66; Pius XII on, 166–67

and working class, 167–71; Leo XIII on, 167–69, 170–71; Pius XII on, 169–70

Totalitarianism, Pius XI on, 76; Pius XII on, 77

Unity
  as property of matrimony, 45–46
  European, 193–95; Pius XII on, 193–95

Wage, just, characteristics of, 151–53; Leo XIII on, 152; Pius XI on, 153

Wage contract, justice of, 151; Pius XI on, 151

Wealth, State and distribution of, 165–67

Worldly goods, man's right to, 8–9; Leo XIII on, 9; Pius XI on, 9; Pius XII on, 9

Youth, education of, mixed jurisdiction concerning, 110–11

A NOTE ON THE TYPE

IN WHICH THIS BOOK WAS SET

This book is set in Caledonia, a Linotype face created in 1939 by W. A. Dwiggins, which is by far one of the best book types created in the last 50 years. It has a simple, hard-working, feet-on-the-ground quality and can be classed as a modern type face with excellent color and good readability. The designer claims Caledonia was created by putting a little of each of Scotch Roman, Bulmer, Baskerville and Bodoni together and producing a lively, crisp-like book type. This book was composed by Progressive Typographers, Inc., York, Pa., printed by the Wickersham Printing Company, of Lancaster, Pa., and bound by Moore and Company of Baltimore. The typography and design of this book are by Howard N. King.